Contents

T4-AIK-936

Front cover: Whitekirk golf club, North Berwick.
Graphic Design: Emma Goodman
Editing & Production: Louise Couper, Louise Stanton
No part of "Scotland Home of Golf" may be published or reproduced
in any form without the prior consent of the publisher.©
Published by Pastime Publications Ltd., 6 York Place, Edinburgh EH1 3EP.
Tel: 0131-556 1105. Fax: 0131-556 1129.
First published by The Scottish Tourist Board 1970.
UK & Worldwide Distribution.
Printed & bound in Scotland.

Introduction

We hope you will find this twenty eighth edition of 'Scotland Home of Golf' as informative and useful as ever.

Television, particularly in its satellite form, is bringing competitive golf to an ever increasing world wide audience. Courses are being opened every week all over the world. Scotland, the country which gave the game its rules and created the tradition is also moving with the times. In the 'Home of Golf' new courses open each year and existing clubs build new or upgrade facilities. The visiting golfer makes all this possible and it is the aim of Scottish Golf to make them extremely welcome. In this commentary on selected courses our golf writer Donald Ford constantly emphasises the social side of golf by complementing his comments on the course with a pithy description of the clubhouse atmosphere.

Thank you for buying our book, may it prove a useful companion, and enjoy both course and clubhouse in 1998.

The Publisher

GREAT
Golfing
Escapes

A first class selection of Golfing Breaks with a warm welcome to all non-golfing partners

▶ *Great Golfing Escapes offer three to seven night stays in quality hotels with access to some of the finest golf courses in Scotland. Whichever you choose you are promised excellent value for money and first rate accommodation with guaranteed tee-off times*

▶ *The breaks are centred around ten hotels in the West Coast, East Coast, North Coast and Fife, and each includes table d'hôte dinner, bed and full Scottish breakfast.*

1

BALGEDDIE HOUSE HOTEL

Superbly located for golfing at St. Andrews and within easy reach of Ladybank, Carnoustie, Dalmahoy, Rosemount and over 90 other fine courses, this beautiful mansion house is set within its own grounds in the centre of the Kingdom of Fife, with Balbirnie Park its nearest golf course just 2 kilometres away. A golfer's paradise - only 35 minutes' drive north of Edinburgh Airport.

Under new ownership, Balgeddie House offers you high standards of comfort and facilities, with friendly service and a restaurant which provides the best of Scottish food, cooked with flair and presented with style. The Paddock Bar stocks an excellent selection of real ales or you may prefer to enjoy a game of pool in the Lodge Bar.

Our "Sporting Special" tariff starts at £50 and includes 3 course dinner with bed and breakfast. We will book tee times or arrange a full golfing programme free of charge.

Tel: (01592) 742511
Fax: (01592) 621702
e-mail:
balgeddie@easynet.co.uk

Balgeddie House Hotel, Balgeddie Way, Glenrothes, Fife KY6 3ET

Scottish Tourist Board COMMENDED ♚ ♣♣♣♣ **RAC** ★ ★ ★ *AA* ★ ★ ★ **Egon Ronay**

Rescobie Hotel

Scottish Tourist Board COMMENDED ♚ ♣♣♣♣ **RAC** ★ ★ *AA* ★ ★

For golfers looking for a home away from home, Rescobie is a charming family-fun hotel which offers you comfort, friendly service and excellent food. Our restaurant has held both an AA Rosette and an RAC Merit Award for the last 5 years and has been a member of the Taste of Scotland for 10 years.

Ideally positioned for a golfing holiday, we are within easy reach of St. Andrews, Ladybank, Carnoustie, Dalmahoy, Rosemount and over 90 other fine courses. Our "Sporting Special" tariff starts at £45 and includes 3-course dinner with bed and breakfast. We will book tee times or arrange a full golfing programme free of charge.

Tel: (01592) 742143 Fax: (01592) 620231 e-mail: rescobie@easynet.co.uk
Rescobie Hotel, Valley Drive, Leslie, Glenrothes, Fife KY6 3BA

BALMORAL GOLF RESERVATIONS

Photograph: Phil Sheldon

St. Andrews
Muirfield
Royal Troon
Carnoustie
Turnberry
Royal Birkdale
Lytham St Annes......

* Pre-Booked Tee Times
* Luxury Accommodation
* Executive Transport

"For golfers who know where they're going"

Balmoral Golf Reservations, Northbank Farm,
St. Andrews, Fife, Scotland KY16 9TZ
Tel: +44 1334 476691. Fax: +44 1334 479450
Email balmoral-golf@sol.co.uk

WHITEKIRK GOLF COURSE
Where everyone is welcome

THE GOLF COURSE

Whitekirk Golf Course is located just outside the historic village of Whitekirk, East Lothian, incorporating quality golfing facilities in a modern golf environment where everyone is made to feel welcome. Comprising of 18 holes, this Par 71 course, has a practice area 300 yds long, and a large putting green and bunker area for the keen golfer to sharpen up their short game. The Clubhouse includes a restaurant, two bars, a golf shop and changing facilities. Whitekirk is open to the public. We encourage golf societies, corporate users and welcome private parties.

Course Features
* USGA specification greens
* automatic watering on greens
* four separate lakes
* many elevated teeing positions
* 360 degree panoramic views over the whole of East Lothian and beyond
* designed with two loops of nine holes
* four teeing positions on each hole
* buggies available for hire
* great natural wildlife habitat

GOLF TUITION

Improve your game with personal tuition from our P.G.A professional. We offer a comprehensive lesson programme for beginners, intermediate and advanced level golfers, video lessons are also available.

THE CLUBHOUSE AND GOLF SHOP

The main lounge is a welcoming room with large windows overlooking the 9th and 18th greens with panoramic views of Tantallon Castle and the Bass Rock. The perfect place to enjoy a morning coffee, light snack or evening meal. There is also a separate spikes bar accessible straight from the course with an open fire for those cold winter days. Well equipped ladies and gents changing rooms with disabled facilities are provided. The clubhouse has a full public house licence enabling it to be open to golfers and non golfers alike. The shop has a comprehensive stock of leading brands of equipment, clothing and accessories. Expert advice available from P.G.A. Golf Professionals. Try before you buy your clubs. Buggy, trolley and club hire available.

ACCOMMODATION

Whitekirk Main Farm quality en-suite Bed & Breakfast available.
Contact Mrs J. Tuer (01620) 870245 / 870300 Fax: (01620) 870330.

LOCATION

Whitekirk lies in the heart of East Lothian and is situated 3 miles off the main A1 Edinburgh-Berwick-upon-Tweed road, on the A198 to the east of North Berwick.

Whitekirk Golf Course, Whitekirk,
Nr. North Berwick, East Lothian EH42 1XS
Tee Reservations: (01620) 870300 Fax: (01620) 870330

Peter Alliss, having been one of the U.K.'s leading professional golfers for many years, represented Britain in the Ryder Cup and enjoyed a large number of tournament victories in the 1960's and 70's. He is acknowledged as being one of the finest coaches in the modern game; now B.B.C. Television's leading commentator at all major championships.

Unforgettable memories

by Peter Alliss

I can remember very clearly the first time I ever visited Scotland. I was with my father and he took me to play in the Boys' Championship at Bruntsfield Links on the west side of Edinburgh. It was round about August/September 1946, I was fifteen years of age and it was the first time I had ever made a long journey - at least one that I could remember. I had travelled as a one year old from Berlin to London in 1932, but memories of that visit are, to say the least, blurred. 1946 was also the first occasion I ever played International Golf as an amateur. I was picked for the England side and the prowess I showed during the match installed me as one of the favourites to win the competition. It wasn't to be, as I was seen off by a little fellow from Manchester called Donald Dunsdan. I returned home to Ferndown, that delightful course some six miles north of Bournemouth and my father made the grand announcement that I wasn't going to be a brain surgeon or a K.C., so the sensible thing would be to become an apprentice to him. This I did and that was the beginning of a long affair with most, if not all, things Scottish.

Although it would be totally wrong to say that golf in Scotland is not elitist, Scotland was the first country I visited where the sight of someone, whatever their age, walking down the High Street, travelling on a bus or train, carrying a set of clubs, was not looked upon as a complete lunatic. Although there were golf clubs that were for

looked upon as a complete lunatic. Although there were golf clubs that were for them (the professional men, the doctors, lawyers, accountants or high powered businessmen) there were plenty of places for "ordinary" folk to play the wondrous game. Still to this day it is possible to find inexpensive golf in Scotland. I recently completed a television series in which I visited Durness, the most northerly golf club in Britain, nine holes totally constructed by the members with the most stunning views. Yes, we were blessed with a calm, beautiful day.

Although the course only had nine holes, there were many challenging shots to be played. It is easy, of course, to mention the famous courses in Scotland where Championships have been played yesterday and today. The wonderful Gleneagles Hotel; Rosemount, where David Thomas and I had the privilege of creating the second course, known as the Lansdowne. I am glad it has turned out to be such a fine test of golf. That wondrous stretch of coastline from Stranraer all the way up past Glasgow where you can almost step from one course to the next creates in each its own divine and devious pleasures. Further north you have Royal Dornoch, Buckie, Banchory, Aboyne, Tain, Nairn - ah! what a little jewel. The courses round Aberdeen provide a wealth of pleasure and Newmachar, another

Newmachar, another course created by David Thomas and myself, is already becoming an inland classic. There are a myriad of choices around Edinburgh. Strike out towards East Lothian and you come to Gullane, the Honourable Company of Golfers at Muirfield, Dunbar, Musselburgh, Aberlady, North Berwick; Fife has Elie, Leven and Lundin Links. The courses along the Clyde, Helensburgh and the magnificent new Loch Lomond complex; up north again to Golspie, Strathpeffer - and what about Boat of Garten? I went there when there was a foot of snow on the ground! I had my friend Michael Hobbs with me on that occasion; we were gathering material for a book which we were putting together at the time and I can remember us following a loan pair of footsteps from the car park to the clubhouse, whose doors were open - not a soul anywhere in sight. I left a message on the table - which I'm sure nobody believed but sometime later I did get a note from the club asking if I had indeed visited it! Any of the aforementioned courses on the west coast on a nice day are absolutely stunning. The history of Prestwick, the majesty of Troon, the delights of Turnberry and its glorious hotel - so many to choose. Nor must we forget golf on the islands, which are all well worth exploring.

Of course things have got more expensive as the years have gone by but, if you really take the trouble to do a little detective work there is something for everyone in Scotland, plus the delights - as Angela Bonallack points out below in this editorial - of small hotels, bed and breakfasts and of course there are the grander hotels waiting to take care of your every whim. Sally forth and enjoy it all.

Scotland - from the ladies' tee

by Angela Bonallack

Angela Bonallack was Britain's top lady golfer between 1956 and 1966, with many tournament victories and honours to her name; despite the requirement for two hip replacement operations, she still golfs regularly - and well - and is actively involved in charity work for the Wishbone Trust. Her husband Michael is secretary to the Royal and Ancient.

What an interesting but demanding project to be handed; an invitation to let lady golfers know how we would enjoy holidaying and golfing in Scotland! There are so many really excellent courses (which do not have the publicity or stature of the "Open" venues) where one may enjoy a really good time - on and off the course. Let me start in the Home of Golf - or rather, Fife. A delightful venue just a few miles east of the Forth Road Bridge is Aberdour. Some fascinating holes, some quite narrow but nearly all adjacent to the sea, with splendid craggy views - features of this little course. Here I would choose to go with, perhaps, another three kindred spirited ladies of similar age and golfing standards, whose husbands are away (probably on some men-only golf week!).We would put our bags into one of the plentiful local clean-looking bed and breakfasts, where hopefully an evening meal would also be available and then, having telephoned the previous week to confirm that the course would be available, off we would go. (Of course, we would have a modest kitty and interchange our pairings!). After our golf, we would look forward to dinner and perhaps a couple of rubbers of bridge. Mind you my companions would need to have a good sense of humour and not be moaners! For day two, we would need to drive only a few miles up the coast to Elie where holes ten, eleven, twelve and thirteen are four of the most picturesque on the eastern Scottish seaboard. Toasties, coffee and a warm welcome in the clubhouse; then we may (strength- and weather-permitting) play Crail on the same afternoon or the next day. A lovely Fife afternoon would then find us on the road to the beautiful "Home of Golf", St. Andrews. Sight-seeing first; the mediaeval University buildings, the bottle dungeon in the old Castle, the St. Rule Tower, where we can climb to the top and take in the great views over the city and beyond to the golf courses. (The largest cathedral ruins in Scotland predominate on the south side). We would not be playing the famous courses this time around, so we would find one of the splendid bed and breakfasts at a farm house outside Newburgh. We will need a morning off at this stage so take ourselves east along the south banks of the Tay, visiting minute villages such as Balmerino with its Gothic church and tiny hilly streets that all seem to end in the river! Now on our fourth day, we will take ourselves over the Tay Bridge towards Blairgowrie on the A93 and turn off to the splendid inland course at Alyth. This is always in great condition and has charming views with the Highlands making a backdrop. Again a great bed and breakfast and another couple of rubbers of bridge and we fall into our beds!

A few miles further east, having passed through some splendid Angus countryside, is Kirriemuir. Here we find a totally different soil, silver birches and heathers and, of course, excellent views all about us. We have an even larger breakfast, not intending to eat again until the evening at an exquisite small restaurant in the village. Five days on, our golf is now becoming very competitive (as is our modest bridge, I must say!). Two of us therefore decide that we need a little help with our golf and find the charming pro' has half an hour the following morning to sort us out. He also has a great range of ladies' golf clothing (a little of most makes) so we make our purchases and don't look as though we're on a school outing! Only a short distance west along the A93 we reach Ballater. This is yet another delightful town with a distinctly Scottish Highland feeling; maybe it is a few degrees cooler but water, mountains, heather, fir trees of all dimensions and superb greens more than compensate. This course usually has snow in winter for several weeks - perhaps this is one of the reasons it is always in such excellent condition (the winter

weather will give it a rest from the golfers). The breathtaking views from the course make it difficult to concentrate on the golf and afterwards there are several very pleasant shops and small eating places in the town where the locals are ever welcoming. For the last day of our golfing holiday we have a difficult choice. We opt to travel north west up the A939 through Tomintoul to Grantown on Spey. Here we have a delightful eighteen hole course, although perhaps the hills are better for younger people! Again we find an idyllic bed and breakfast, enjoy our final evening of bridge and then we head south at the end of a week's wonderful holiday, remembering the laughs, the comfortable accommodation (and our most expensive green fee of £27.) Our whole week's holiday (with one day of golf), seven bed and breakfasts and a golf lesson thrown in would probably come to a grand total of £260 plus petrol and food - what a great time could be had for that amount of money!

Let me close with a plea to those who run the game in Scotland. I feel that we lose out on many potential golfing visitors through our own reluctance to allow single ride-on buggies. It has been proved that the single battery operated buggy, which may be dismantled easily by two ladies into three pieces (plus the batteries) do more damage to courses than a player wearing metal spikes and pushing one of the many varieties of mechanised golf carts. I myself, who choose to always use a three wheel ride-on buggy (having had two hips replaced) would enjoy taking a holiday like this but at 60 years old I could not contemplate such a venture. Think of the fun such people could have if only someone would put this suggestion in front of the powers that be. Maybe even if you needed to, private buggies could be allowed for people over sixty or those with a health condition that necessitates it? (It's time I had a word with my husband!) I do hope the considered criticism within those last few paragraphs does not dampen the enthusiasm of all you lady golfers who may be thinking about a week or two in Scotland. You will, I have no doubt, find it an unforgettable experience, both from a golfing and a social point of view.

For anyone interested in playing the ancient game of golf - Dumfries & Galloway must be high on their list of places to visit. There are over thirty golf clubs in the region - all happy to welcome visitors. They range from 18 hole championship links courses, to 9 hole upland courses where you can enjoy a relaxed and pleasant round of golf while taking in some of the most delightful scenery the region has to offer. Many of the courses are such a haven for wildlife that it is sometimes difficult to concentrate on the golf! If you fancy some practice before your round there are a number of driving ranges in the region providing this facility. The Dumfries and Galloway Tourist Board are operating a 'Gateway to Golf' pass scheme which you will find easy to use and make your golf even more cost effective. Explanatory leaflets along with three day and five day books of tickets are available from the following tourist information centres when you arrive in the area:

Well, she did say somewhere with plenty of sand.

Colvend Course, on Solway Coast.

Visit Dumfries & Galloway and you'll be amazed at the variety offered by our 31 golf courses. From the tradition of the seaside links courses, to the lush parkland courses nestling in rolling hills, you'll find many of them are of tournament standard.

To let you enjoy these courses to the full we have a discount package, known as the Gateway to Golf Pass. You can play two rounds a day, for either 3 or 5 days, at the course of your choice, for a fraction of the normal price.

When will you go? The region also benefits from the Gulf Stream which brings mild weather all year round. At the l hostelries visitors get a welcome that's just as warm. These pack deals show excellence is par for the course.

Fernhill Hotel, Portpatrick. Tel: 01776 810220. Very l for Dunskey Golf Club. Special midweek and weekend breaks available.

The Pheasant Hotel, Dalbeattie. Tel: 01556 610345. The R Hotel, Kirkcudbright. Tel: 01557 331213. Excellent accommoda and catering. Golf packages available.

Newton Stewart Golf Club. Tel: 01671 402172. 18 hole cor

SCOTLAND

Castle Douglas, Dalbeattie, Dumfries, Gatehouse of Fleet, Gretna Gateway, Gretna Green, Kirkcudbright, Langholm, Moffat, Newton Stewart, Sanqhuar, and Stranraer. The 3 day pass costs £65 per person and the 5 day pass costs £95 per person. Purchase golf passes in advance by sending your name, the dates of your holiday and the appropriate remittance (cheques payable to Dumfries & Galloway Tourist Board) to:
Tourist Information Centre, Whitesands, Dumfries DG1 2RS.

For parties of two or more, please note that all the names of those playing will be required. Visa and Access bookings are acceptable by telephone - please contact (01387) 253862 which is the advance telephone booking point all year round.

If you would like a copy of the Dumfries & Galloway Tourist Board Holiday and Accommodation Guide simply call the Brochure Request Line on: (0990) 134948 (calls are charged at local rates.) For more complete information on any other outdoor activities, ask at any Tourist Information Centre for guides to Fishing, Gardens, Walking, Cycling and Field Sports in Dumfries & Galloway.

scenic views of Galloway Hills and Wigtown Bay. Excellent
ring. Visitors (including groups) welcome.
&B, Castle Douglas. Tel: 01556 650233. Friendly family run
century farmhouse. All rooms en-suite. Log fires. Fresh local
luce. Taste of Scotland.
o find out more about what makes
nfries & Galloway the perfect
way fill in the coupon or call
0 134948, or see our website
ww.galloway.co.uk

Dumfries & Galloway

If Scotland is the home of golf, then the Highlands provide the highlights. In just a small area a few miles north of Inverness there are a wealth of outstanding courses. Centred on the legendary Royal Dornoch course, the district boasts no fewer than 9 excellent-18 hole courses within a 30 minute driving radius. Although far enough north for play at midnight on mid-summer's day, the area benefits from the lowest rainfall in Scotland and the highest number of sunshine hours - comparable to the south coast of England.

The cathedral town of Dornoch has two courses, the 6514 yard Championship course, designed by Tom Morris and the 5438 yard Struie course. Handicap certificates are required for the former and booking can be difficult, but the Struie course is readily accessible. The nearby Carnegie Club course at Skibo Castle was laid out for Andrew Carnegie, the Scottish/American steel tycoon in 1898, by John Sutherland, then secretary at Royal Dornoch. The Carnegie Club is now a private members club, but can be played by visitors on a "once only" day membership basis. In August 1991, Dornoch gained a significant golfing partner - the opening of the Dornoch Bridge, meant that the other Tom Morris designed course at Tain, was only 10 minutes drive away. The availabilty of two such excellent courses in such close proximity gives golfers considerable flexibility in planning their itineraries. The Tain course was designed in 1890 and is a typical Scottish links course, with whins, bent grass and natural bunkers. It includes the Tain River which introduces challenges at the 2nd and 16th holes. With holes playing in each direction of the compass, the changing winds add variety through-out the course. Greens are invariably in immaculate condition, carefully tended by Ian Macleod, Scotland's Greenkeeper of the Year 1993.

Also in Tain are a number of attractions for golfers and non-golfers alike. The world famous Glenmorangie whisky Distillery has a modern

Visitor's Centre and provides an excellent conducted tour and whisky tasting. Tain Through Time is a museum complex which traces the history of this, the oldest Royal Burgh in Scotland. A working water mill and pottery are among the other attractions the town has to offer, and accommodation needs are well provided for by the Mansfield House Hotel, a 5 Crown country house hotel which is rapidly gaining a reputation as one of the leading hotels in the Highlands.

North of Dornoch are two other fine courses at Brora and Golspie. Both are by the sea and designed by James Braid. The Brora course is higher above sea level and on a clear day affords magnificent views over the North Sea and the far distant oil and gas platforms. Between the two courses lies the impressive Dunrobin Castle, the family home of the Dukes of Sutherland.

Three nine hole courses at Bonar Bridge, Portmahomack and Alness surround Tain to the east, west and south, and visitors to the Portmahomack course can also visit the Tarbat Discovery Centre, a Pictish site which is currently undergoing excavation.

In the near vicinity is the new 18 hole course at Invergordon, the site of the famous mutiny, and a port which is becoming a favoured stopping-off point for cruiseliners. On the other side of the Cromarty Firth is the peninsular course of Fortrose and Rosemarkie, where badly struck balls mimic seagulls in their dives for water.

Finally, and by complete contrast is the upland course of Strathpeffer. It is a short, but hilly course close to the Victorian Spa town, where golf is accompanied by breathtaking views of the mountains of Kintail.

Mansfield House Hotel

All of these courses are within no more than 40 minutes drive from the Mansfield House Hotel in Tain. Once the private residence of the turn-of-the-century Provost of Tain, the house is a magnificent baronial mansion, with extensive wood panelling and ornate plaster ceilings. Under new ownership since 1995, the public rooms and the 8 bedrooms which have also been carefully restored in period style, with antique furniture and modern conveniences.

A modern wing of the house has a further 10 bedrooms which have also been newly refurbished and have the flexibility of having twin beds which zip-link to form king-sized doubles. Rated 5 Crown for its facilities, which include a beauty salon and massage suite, and Highly Commended for the quality of the service, the hotel is listed in such fine guides as Michelin, Taste of Scotland and the Which Guide. Fowler's Restaurant, which draws extensively on fresh local meat, game and fish, has received two special awards, and the bar is well stocked with a wide range of malt whiskies, including Glenmorangie, and two real ales from a Highland Brewery. Mansfield House achieved Investors in People status in only 10 months, and the staff exclude hospitality - for which they received merit awards from the R.A.C. and Les Routiers.

A member of the Scotland's Commended Consortium, the hotel can arrange special golf packages, tee-off times and discounted green fees at some clubs.

Information on the hotel can be had by telephoning (01862) 892052.

Drumoig arrives - and Scottish golf moves forward

Jim Farmer has, for many years, been one of the leading Professionals on Scotland's Tartan Tour. Recognised as one of the finest coaches in the Scottish game, he has now taken a position as Director of Golf at the Scottish Golf Union's new National Training Centre at Drumoig, just west of St. Andrews.

by Jim Farmer

Drumoig enjoys the good fortune in having been selected by the S.G.U. and the S.G.L.A., not only to house the administrative base for their organisations, but also to operate as Scotland's National Training Centre for golf. As a result, Drumoig has been catapulted into the golfing arena, achieving a much higher level than if it had stood alone in the market place. It was John Foster, Chairman and creator of Drumoig, who had the vision to see the impact the development would have on this deeply historic area, only seven miles from St. Andrews, the "Home of Golf".

Drumoig is surrounded by world renowned championship courses such as Carnoustie, St. Andrews, Downfield, Rosemount and Gleneagles. There are also many new courses such as the Duke's, Letham Grange and Murrayshall all within easy striking distance. For those golfers who are looking for a less challenging round we also have a selection of courses in the vicinity. Scotscraig, Lundin Links, Ladybank, Elie and Crail, each has its own characteristics and - in the case of the first three, the pedigree of Open Qualifying courses. To be able to slot into the heart of such a selection of wonderful courses gives Drumoig a huge advantage in selling itself as one of Europe's leading golf courses. Special emphasis is being placed on education and training for the game of golf. Scotland, of course, has been at the forefront of world golf since the game began. Until now we have been forced to train our up-and-com-

ing golfers in poor Scottish winter weather. At Drumoig, however, we are addressing the problem by creating a purpose-built indoor and outdoor arena where up-and-coming golfers can develop their skills and knowledge - as is now happening all over Europe. It would be naive to believe that our natural talent would be enough to see us through the developing European game, leaving Scotland behind us as our friends across the Channel succeed in discovering the necessary structures to make the most of their own golfing talents. The coaching of young golfers has been gradually improving over the years but is solely reliant on good club professionals. The S.G.U. intends to structure each and every Junior Section to maximise the potential of Junior golf in Scotland.

We must improve technique by laying firm ground rules on grip, stance, aim and posture with solid swing planes. Hopefully, then, with this in place, National Coaching can concentrate on preparing our charges for tournament golf and instill the mental skills required to cope and perform at the top level. Everyone at Drumoig - myself included - is very excited at the prospects for Scottish golf created by this terrific new development. What price a new young Scottish golfer winning the Open Championship by 2001?!

Carnoustie returns to the top

by Donald Ford

With the possible exception of those professionals who love nothing better than the pursuit of trophies on lush parkland and soft holding greens, there was sheer delight when the R & A announced that the Open was going back to Carnoustie in 1999.

These famous links, where famous legends Ben Hogan, Gary Player and Tom Watson have enjoyed the ultimate success, thoroughly merit this recall - many would say it is overdue - to the Championship rota. Over the past three or four years, under the watchful and creative eye of John Philp, the course has grown in stature and subtle improvements have made it an even harder test for the best in the world - and if the wind blows?! There is one sadness about it all; John Calder, who more than anyone else worked tirelessly to convince the "powers that be" that Carnoustie was worthy of recall, will not be there to see the fruits of all his labours during the 1990's. "Jock"

passed away in 1996. It is not easy to convey the atmosphere of the course, the degree of difficulty or the sheer brilliance of James Braid's design through ground-level camera work. However, back to golf and to the difficult task of whetting, in but a few paragraphs, the appetite of the reader for Carnoustie. It is acknowledged world wide that the start is stiff and the degree of difficulty of playing to handicap accelerates as the round continues. From hole fourteen to eighteen, the course possesses the hardest finish anywhere in Championship Golf. In fact, your round could be over by the sixth if things don't go well. The new hidden bunker at the front of the first green makes a mid or long iron approach (dependent on the wind) highly dangerous. Number two "(Gulley)" needs two absolutely straight shots of about 400 yards to allow two putts for par on a big, difficult green. "Jocky's Burn", the third, requires a laid-up drive to avoid left-sided and central bunkers, then a high but short approach to a bigger,

1st green: Yet another escape required from the new bunker to the front right of the green - invisible for the second shot.

rolling green which literally begins at the ditch. Holes four and five perhaps allow some latitude, but no lapse in concentration. "Daunting" is an adjective which totally understates the feeling one gets on the sixth tee. 490 yards for the club golfer, but a massive 566 yard hike for the professional, there are roughly 35 yards' width to land the drive. An out-of-bounds fence goes all the way from tee to green down the left; "Hogan's Alley" (if you are brave enough to use it!) is a twenty yard gap between the said fence and the central fairway bunkers to catch the drive. The second shot must avoid a ditch and if you are not in pole position to hit the flag with your approach, five greenside and one rear bunker will finish you off!

You might well therefore be driving on the 7th (out-of-bounds again from tee to green on the left) with nothing but a rescue operation in mind. It is not the easiest place to launch a lifeboat; bunkers aplenty and - oddly for Carnoustie - a fairly small putting surface. The short eighth brings some welcome relief from the driver; 147 yards from the front tee, out of bounds plus bunkers around a narrow sloping green make this, however, another hole which demands accuracy and quality putting. Jack Nicklaus was critical of the 401- yard ninth; so much so that another bunker now threatens a drive too far right. Otherwise a long iron or wood needs to find a fairly straight route to the long, narrow green, which is more than adequately protected by bunkers. "South America", the 415 yard tenth hole, begins a potentially frightening back nine. The drive position is crucial; too far left makes the second an almost impossible proposition, particularly if pin position is anything left of centre and therefore hiding behind two comprehensive greenside bunkers. The course of the Barry Burn some forty yards from the green makes club selection for the second shot confusing - even if you choose correctly, the burn loops right around the landing area and will catch anything wayward.

Eleven, twelve and thirteen probably provide the last chance to pick up a birdie. If you are standing on the fourteenth tee requiring to make up lost ground, forget it. From now until the clubhouse you are fighting to extract par figures from the five most demanding finishing holes in the world. A new bunker in front of the invisible fourteenth green claims the vast majority of straight but under-hit approach shots assuming your ball successfully avoids "The Spectacles" in the first place. Hole fifteen "Lucky Slap" needs yet another long iron approach - when was the last time eight, nine or pitching wedge was used?! Fifteenth green is flat but massive, needing quality putting. So to the 223 yard sixteenth which, to the amateur, is the equivalent of an Everest climb without oxygen. Bunkers to right and left, an uninviting entrance over typical bumpy links to a narrow green sloping up from front to back, render the expedition to find green from tee almost flukish. Then you have, probably, one putt on a devilish slope to save par.

Against the prevailing westerlies, getting on board the seventeenth green in two is difficult; avoiding the burn from the tee is only the first obstacle. Four bunkers endanger the wayward approach and the green lies low in a surrounding gorse bank to further complicate a long second shot. With the extension of the eighteenth to 512 yards from the medal tee, an extremely difficult par 4 could be a less onerous five. Provided the drive is straight, the second pulls up short of the second loop of the Barry Burn and an accurate pitch follows to a carefully trapped green you might even generate a birdie chance - but don't count on it. The 6,405 yards (7,187 for the professionals) will either leave you very tired or very exhilarated. Irrespective it is unlikely that you will forget the challenges of this immense golf course.

It is absolutely right that Carnoustie will, next year, bid welcome to the greatest golfers in the world once again. How the big names will cope with it, especially if the weather misbehaves, is a fascinating prospect. I hope the foregoing paragraphs have whetted your appetite, either to come and sample the atmosphere yourself, or at least not to miss the coverage next year as the greatest links in Britain welcome back The Open.

SOUTH AYRSHIRE

Home of Good Golf

...yrshire, you are never very far from a ... course. And as any golfer knows, some ...e courses along the 30 mile "Golf Coast" ... rated among the finest in the world. Names ... Royal Troon, Turnberry, which regularly hosts the 'open' ... of course, Prestwick Old Course which hosted the first ...en' in 1860, stir the imagination and enthusiasm of novice ... professional golfers alike.

...ally challenging and each with its own particular charac-
... South Ayrshire's eight municipal courses, three of which
... of championship standard, are not to be missed.

...r more information contact:
...tegic Services, Burns House,
...ns Statue Square, Ayr, KA7 1UT
...01292 616270 Fax: 01292 616161

Belleisle
Belleisle Park, Ayr Tel: 01292 441258

Seafield
Belleisle Park, Ayr Tel: 01292 441258

Dalmilling
Westwood Avenue, Ayr Tel: 01292 263893

Girvan
Golf Course Road, Girvan Tel: 01465714346

Lochgreen
Harling Drive, Troon Tel: 01292 312464

Darley
Harling Drive, Troon Tel: 01292 312464

Fullarton
Harling Drive, Troon Tel: 01292 312464

Maybole
Memorial Park, Maybole Tel: 01292 616270

south
AYRSHIRE
COUNCIL

Donald Ford in the Home of Golf

Donald Ford, our regular contributor, has produced a wonderful collection of views which demonstrate vividly the beauty and diversity of Scotland's courses For some of these shots he had to get up very early in the morning, but as he said, he always found someone on the course! Donald makes a lot of friends as he tours around the clubs and you will find this reflected in his comments. We are sure you will find his guidance practical and helpful and will share his views.

The best ever - with more to come...

The weather forecast the previous evening had promised a clear night, a bright dawn and at least a morning's duration of sunshine. Gleneagles, I knew, would be looking a picture just a couple of weeks before the Ladies' Championship. I was understandably excited at the prospect of some great shots of Scotland's most panoramic inland course. My 5am arrival for sunrise at Gleneagles was misplaced optimism at its very best! Flat grey sky, not the slightest chance of a solitary ray of sun - so by 6.30 a.m. and some two to three miles' perambulation of the King's and Queen's courses, it wasn't any better. Yet again, I silently cursed our chameleon weather, abandoned ship and headed for home. There were other disappointments around "The Home of Golf" over the year, but they were far outweighed by the pleasure of visiting and enjoying some seventy or eighty of our courses, from the best known to the "hidden gems".

The appearance and condition of links, parkland and heath continues to excite and please club member visitor and photographer! Advances in course equipment and another impressive leap in green keeping standards have combined to produce the best looking venues for golf we have ever witnessed in Scotland. It is perhaps unfair to single out Loch Lomond and Gleneagles for being outstandingly prepared because financial resources ensure that the very best of equipment and labour is available. Fairways were manicured, beautifully mown

and you could putt on them. Greens were like snooker tables. Off-course facilities were five star. At the other end of the scale one cannot praise too highly the efforts of the Kirkcudbrights, the Stonehavens, the Melroses, the Colvends, the Rothesays, to name but a few, whose courses looked quite superb in 1997 and deserve all the support and plaudits which members and visitors heap on them. Golfing visitors continue to flood in to the "Home of Golf" and to be boastful, it is hardly surprising. We now must possess the richest seam of golfing venues anywhere in the world and, amazingly it seems, each year they reach greater heights. For the fifth year in a row I say to those readers who know what I'm talking about - haste ye back! To the ones who have yet to see it all, make it in 1998.

My first thanks must go again to secretaries, stewards, greenkeepers, members, visitors and others who have all made my photography of the Scottish golfing scene such a pleasurable experience. If I upset anyone by my presence among you I apologise. I do know that the presence of the camera ensured on several occasions a birdie putt or a great bunker recovery; at least, I am taking the credit for them all! I would also like to express my sincere thanks to our guest writers for this year's handbook, all of whose knowledge and skills in the game of golf are widely acclaimed and whose contributions to the editorial are both entertaining and highly informative.

Lauder

Created in 1896 on heath west of the town, an unusually long nine holer where accuracy off the tee and quality irons are keys to a successful round. Superb eastward views to the town, Thirlestane Castle and lovely Border countryside.
6,002 yards, par 72.

Innerleithen

Hidden away on the B709 road to Heriot, this is a mainly flat nine hole layout but littered with hazards, like Leithen Water, not a few ditches - and the road!
Excellent holiday golf in typical Border country.
5,984 yards, par 68.

Lauder: A fine view eastwards and down to the town from the edge of the 6th green (par 3, 150 yards)

Innerleithen: The ditch, the road and Leithen Water combine to bring trouble galore to an excellent opening par 3.

Melrose

A beautifully maintained nine hole course on the northern slopes of the Eildon Hills. A few steepish slopes to contend with but the quality of presentation and the location ensure its continuing popularity as a holiday venue.
5,579 yards, par 68.

St. Boswells

Acknowledged as one of the favourite nine hole courses in southern Scotland. Situated above and on the banks of the Tweed, it is a layout whose short irons will make or break your score. Friendship personified in the clubhouse.
5,250 yards, par 65.

Melrose: Looking down the 5th; precision patterns on newly mown fairways epitomise this lovely 9 hole layout.

St. Boswells: The view from the 1st fairway towards the par 3, 2nd green, the Tweed and lovely Borders country beyond.

Minto: The peak of Ruberslaw dominates the southerly skyline on the inward 9. Here it shows in a downhill view of the 11th.

Minto

A beautiful parkland course on the southern slopes of the Minto Hills just five minutes from Hawick. A superb clubhouse complements a most attractive layout which makes use of every natural feature. One or two climbs but not a strenuous experience by any means (no par 5's) and lovely views yet again.
5,460 yards, par 68.

Selkirk

Yet another nine hole Border course, hilly but perfectly manageable, where accuracy is absolutely essential if repeated battles with heather are to be avoided! The dog-leg fifth is a cracking hole and the monstrous eighth will test the best.
5,620 yards, par 68.

The Roxburghe

Dave Thomas' creation has already received rapturous approval from amateur and professional alike and justifiably so. Now reaching maturity this is a terrific and demanding course whose length and design will be a severe test for the very best golfer, let alone the enthusiastic amateur. Superb food and hospitality will compensate.
6,531 yards, (daily tees), par 72.

Moffat

One of the best situations in the Borders - for golf as well as scenery. On the hill west of the town, in lovely condition and boasting a design by Ben Sayers. The accent is firmly on the short game which will make or break a score. Another friendly clubhouse will make a visit here a memorable experience.
5,218 yards, par 69.

Selkirk: Looking down the par 4, 5th towards the stepped green; a dog leg makes this difficult hole even more awkward.

The Roxburghe: Water and bunkers galore await the errant tee shot at the demanding par 3, 13th (183 yards)

Moffat: Unsurpassed views of the Southern Uplands from all over the course. Here early sun lights up the 14th green.

Braehead

The popular eighteen holes just outside Alloa where a stiff inward nine requires the golfer to take advantage of the outward half (500 yards shorter with several birdie opportunities at shortish par 4's). An excellent clubhouse completes the picture.
5,747 yards, par 70.

Muckhart

A much sought after venue for outings and holiday golf in an idyllic location below the Ochil Hills. Lovely natural features around the course, from rolling fairway to heather, trees and ditches - and great variety in the layout. A second course (opening soon) testifies to the popularity of this venue.
5,800 yards, par 71.

Aberfoyle

A short, but highly entertaining eighteen holes - epecially on a lovely summer day in the Trossachs. Lots of opportunities to prove how good your irons are and small greens demand accurate approach play and good putting. A classic holiday course.
4,810 yards, par 66.

Glenbervie

One of Scotland's finest parkland courses, this is an extremely tough test of even the lowest handicapped. One of the most demanding finishes around (from the par 3, 13th to the 18th there are two par 5's and one of the best par 4's - the 14th - in Scotland). superb hospitality and a marvellous clubhouse; with the presence of John Chillas, one of Scotland's best club Professionals, this is a great day's sport.
5,983 yards, par 71.

Braehead: looking back from the 16th green; a teasing 270 yards par 4 which precedes a hard finish!

Muckhart: The splash of gorse and the Ochils dominate; this view is of the 11th green "Windy Ridge"

Aberfoyle: Not the best Scottish golfing weather in the Trossachs! This shot looks north west over the 16th green.

Glenbervie: Wonderful broad-leaved trees proliferate; here the hilltop clubhouse is framed by a monster on the fifteenth.

Powfoot

Typical Scottish links set out on the Solway Firth, west of Annan. A first class test of all the golfer's skills on a seaside layout and if the wind blows up the Firth it is a really trying eighteen holes. It is a great favourite for "just over the Border" visits.

6,266 yards, par 70.

Southerness

Recognised at last as a high quality links course and now rewarded with more and more tournaments. Superbly designed by MacKenzie Ross only fifty years ago, the dog-leg twelfth must be one of the best par 4's in Scottish links golf. This popular course demands pre-booking.

6,105 yards, par 70.

Powfoot: Appropriately titled "Sand Hole", the par 3, 154 yard 7th demands absolute accuracy to avoid seven greenside bunkers.

Southerness: Early mist on Criffel in this view north from the green of the dog-leg par 4, 12th arguably the best of a superb 18 holes.

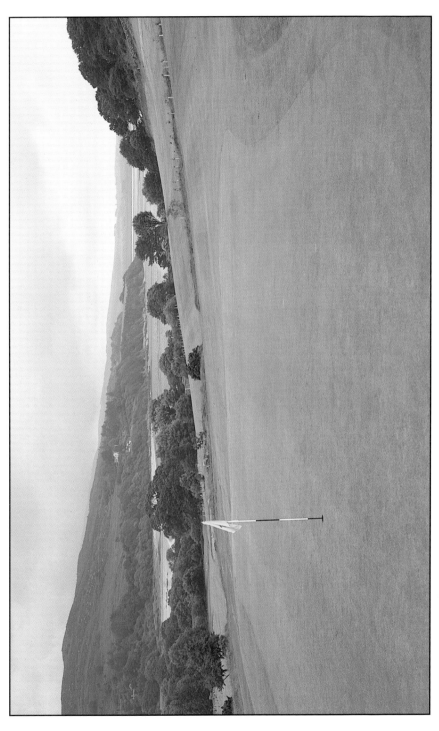

Colvend: Looking west down the 6th towards Sandyhills Bay; a straightforward, though uphill, par 4 (328 yards)

Kirkcudbright: The view to the town from the edge of the 15th fairway across the par 3, 16th (181 yards)

Colvend

Upgraded to eighteen holes in 1997, this is arguably the best and most friendly holiday course in the south of Scotland. In perfect condition when I paid my visit with the camera and at £50 for a weekly ticket the epitome of value for money holiday golf, amidst great scenery and hospitality.

4,716 yards, par 68

Kirkcudbright

Yet another terrific D & G golfing gem; highly popular with visitors - welcomed at weekends - and superb parkland layout for £20 per day. In near perfect condition now and an ideal base for a week's golf around the Region.

5,739 yards, par 69.

Wigtownshire County

True "flat" links golf on the shores of Luce Bay ensure the popularity - and difficulty - of this excellent eighteen holes. The almost permanent presence of the wind adds spice to a course which demands much of your irons and of your putting on subtly sloping greens.
5,535 yards, par 70.

St. Medans

The most southerly course in Scotland and one of the most picturesque. Only the sixth hole stretches beyond 300 yards (there are eight par 3's) so it is a total test of irons and putters! The lovely location on a quiet stretch of the coast means that there is normally no rush and plenty time for a relaxed holiday golfing experience.
4,454 yards, par 64.

Portpatrick

Golf World rated this the best holiday course in Southern Scotland and it's easy to see why. Fabulous location, wonderful layout, great views and always kept in absolute peak condition. Be warned - this is a very busy venue and booking is essential.
5,882 yards, par 68.

Portpatrick: A general southerly aspect of one of Scotland's favourite - busiest - holiday courses.

Wigtownshire County: Stormy weather on the horizon as typical Solway winds stir the flag on the 3rd green (358 yards).

St. Medans: One of Scottish golfs prettiest views; across the 7th green towards Monreith Bay, from the elevated fourth tee.

Fife

Aberdour: Splendid sunshine lights up the 1st green and 2nd tee; two terrific par 3's to start your round.

Aberdour

The first - and one of the best - of the south Fife coastal courses; extended to eighteen holes a few years ago with some wonderful par 3's (the second being one of the best in Scotland); tight in places too, but always offering superb views across the Forth.
5,460 yards, par 66.

Elie

One of the most popular courses around the East Neuk of Fife and deservedly so. Superb links, excellent design and normally sea breezes to compound difficult shot selection. One of the lovely villages of this Fife coast, the town and Kincraig Bay are picturesque backdrops to an excellent test of golf.
6,241 yards, par 70.

Elie: Great views over the town to the Isle of May from the high ground west of the links.

Duke's Course

Opened in 1997 and already threatening to steal some of the glory from the links of nearby St. Andrews. A lovely course, skillfully designed by former Open Champion Peter Thomson, this is a lengthy and challenging eighteen holes where he has allied natural features of rolling parkland to his golfing architectural qualities.

6,749 yards, par 72.

Duke's Course: Already attracting rave notices, the new St. Andrews' course is alight with gorse in full bloom.

Drumoig

The new home of the Scottish Golf Union and the most exciting development in Scottish golf for many years. Four par 5's and four long par 3's emphasise the need for concentration off the tee. Resident professional Jim Farmer, the S.G.U.'s Director of Golf, is in charge of a venue which will soon be up with the best.
6,476 yards, par 72.

Drumoig: Lovely reflections of the new clubhouse above the 18th green of the S.G.U.'s new headquarters.

Grampian

Stonehaven

Perhaps the most beautiful club venue I photographed in 1997. Glorious weather and location apart this little course is in majestic condition; the eighteen holes make for perfect holiday golf with the accent mostly on accuracy of short iron-play to smallish greens. Lovely clubhouse facilities too and the views are stunning.
4,804 yards, par 64.

Royal Aberdeen

High quality Championship links at the estuary of the Don, the Balgownie course is an absolute cracker which will impose the most severe examination on any golfer. Bordered by the dunes of the North Sea, Scottish links at their most tricky - and rewarding. One of the oldest and most highly respected by amateur and professional.
6,372 yards, par 71.

Stonehaven: A tropical look on a wonderful July afternoon has the manicured fifth fairway contrasting vividly with the sea beyond.

Royal Aberdeen: Early morning on the classic links of Balgownie.
The view to the clubhouse from the back of the 1st green.

Newburgh-on-Ythan

Not yet in the Cruden Bay class, but a recent extension to eighteen holes and a planned new clubhouse show the ambitions here. Accuracy is paramount as heather proliferates; the generally heath-type fairways are tight in places but this is a real holiday course in a lovely location which in time will prove a money spinner.
5,750 yards, par 70

Cruden Bay

Deservedly in a short list of six for " best British holiday golf course", this is a fabulous links course, cut out of the massive dunes behind the Bay with one classic hole after another. The 507 yard sixth "Bluidy Burn" is an absolute brute into the wind and the short fourth must be one of the best in Scotland. Classic links golf, blessed with above sunshine too.
6,022 yards, par 70

McDonald G.C., Ellon

One of the lesser lights of inland Aberdeenshire courses but a pleasant tree lined eighteen holes with a very stiff outward nine which can make or break your round. Lovely in Autumn as the broad leaved trees around the back nine change colour and a super clubhouse provides first class hospitality.
5,651 yards, par 70.

Old Meldrum

One of the friendliest and most enjoyable clubs in Grampian; the course was extended to eighteen holes some ten years ago and from the yellow tees is of modest length. Tightish fairways and small greens lay the emphasis firmly on accuracy. Superb views over Aberdeenshire and a real warm welcome in the clubhouse.
5,442 yards, par 68.

Newburgh-on-Ythan: Summer at its best in Buchan! Here it lights up the green of the 148 yard 16th.

Cruden Bay: One of the best short holes in Scotland; the 193 yard 4th - total carry from tee to elevated green.

Old Meldrum: 260 yards from the back tee to the 1st green. "We're yokit", it's called, but the westward view is worth the sweat!

McDonald G.C., Ellon: Trees threaten to engulf the inward nine! This view looks through to the green of the long par 4, 17th.

Keith

Close to the "Whisky Trail" and more of a holiday stopping-off town between Aberdeen and Inverness; the golf course however is as attractive as any and well worth a visit. Springy, holding fairways, an attractive layout and nice location are equally rewarding; very modest green fees are a bonus!

5,811 yards, par 68.

Cullen

Beautifully situated around and above the sands of Cullen Bay, this is a short but most exhilarating golfing experience. Short irons will be working overtime and numerous par 3's will thoroughly test accuracy. If it is not happening for you, relax and enjoy a most magnificent panorama.

4,610 yards, par 62.

Keith: A view of the 2nd green and the left-sided bunker which traps so many approaches!

Cullen: Looking down over the 1st and 17th greens to the clubhouse and town beyond.

Boat of Garten

One of the most popular Highland courses, with tight birch lined fairways, natural slopes and hazards and superb scenic views. A lovely clubhouse (and the steam trains!) complete a perfect location for a golfing break. The Club Centenary is 1998 - so the course will be busier then ever.

5,837 yards, par 69.

Machrie

It's a long way to go but worth every penny! A superb links course cut out of the machair on Islay's south-west coastline. Small greens make for accurate iron play; if the golf is "off" just enjoy some of Scotland's most magnificent scenery.

4,677 yards, par 66.

Boat of Garten: The par 3, 1st hole and clubhouse from behind the green; a great start to a superb Highland course.

Machrie: The 5th green and hotel complex, a couple of bunkers and plenty sand dunes!

Royal Dornoch

Held by many to be the best links in the north of Scotland, only its distance from the main population centres prevents greater involvement in the tournament circuit. A typical seaside location and layout but tough going if the wind blows.
6,581 yards par 72.

Isle of Harris

The little nine hole course at Scarista, on south Harris, is cut out of the machair above some of the loveliest white beaches on the western Hebridean seaboard. Fun golf guaranteed - especially if the Atlantic westerlies blow up and it's more than likely you will have it all to yourself!
About 4,800 yards, par 66.

Shiskine (Arran)

A spectacular experience on Arran's west coast, the twelve holes at Shiskine represent holiday links golf at its best. A breathtaking layout featuring seven par 3's, blind tee shots and approaches and extremely fast fairways if the weather has been kind in July and August.
2,823 yards, par 42.

Royal Dornoch: August wild flowers make a colourful foreground behind the 1st green.

Isle of Harris: The second green, from which unrivalled views (westwards to the Atlantic and north to white beaches and the Harris hills) are stunning.

Shiskine: The 8th green ("Hades") with "The Shelf" towering in the background; a ladies foursome enjoying this unique Arran venue.

Kilspindie

A wonderful holiday course, especially for a full day's golf or as part of a week's tour in East Lothian. A hard start (3,5,4,4) - all against the wind - is daunting but then the course is of modest length and in a lovely location, (the views are superb). Handy too, for the city of Edinburgh. 5,410 yards, par 66.

Whitekirk

In a superb location and with an exciting layout, this new East Lothian course is a sure fire hit for member or visitor. A mix of heath and parkland and no pushover for any handicap if the wind gets up. Lovely clubhouse facilities too and enjoying some of Scotland's driest and sunniest conditions.
6,201 yards, par 71

Longniddry

Former host to the Seniors' Championship, this is another East Lothian venue which has a lovely mix of links and parkland. Some terrific holes, notably the dog-legged fifth, short thirteenth and par 4 fourteenth. 6,219 yards, par 70.

Kilspindie: Glorious late afternoon sun lights up the 17th green; not a few have come to grief at the wall!

Whitekirk: Looking towards North Berwick Law from the 11th.

Longniddry: Looking up the short 6th; a cracking little par 3 where club selection is everything.

Gifford: Classic siting of the green fifty yards past the ditch demands a well struck iron at the 2nd hole.

Haddington: Major features of this popular East Lothian course are the mature trees; this pair are sentries to the 16th green.

Newbattle: One of Midlothian's most attractive courses; here the 2nd green - and not a few of the countless trees - feature.

Gifford

This lovely East Lothian village now boasts two courses (Castle Park is new and will in time be a great attraction). The little nine hole course west of the village is the epitome of holiday golf; nothing strenuous, some challenging holes, notably the 2nd and a friendly welcome in the clubhouse and within the village itself.
6,243 yards, par 70.

Haddington

Lush fairways and huge broad leaved trees are the main characteristics of a most enjoyable eighteen holes in the east of the town. Not one of the best known East Lothian venues but well worth a visit.
6,280 yards, par 70.

Newbattle

One of the many excellent Midlothian venues with a wonderful variety of holes, terrific use of natural features (particularly the trees) and clubhouse hospitality second to none. Situated to the south of Dalkeith and astride the River Esk.
6,025 yards, par 69.

Prestonfield

Right in the heart of Edinburgh's south side; overlooked by the huge volcanic hulk of Arthur's Seat, but enjoying a lovely situation and an excellent test of golf. Another warm welcome guaranteed in the excellent clubhouse.
6,216 yards, par 70.

Torphin Hill

One of three courses enjoying an idyllic location on the north facing slopes of the Pentland Hills, Torphin's little course is a gem. Wonderful views, some stiff climbs and drops, but enjoyable sport on a well-presented course where your short iron play will need to work hard!
5020 yards, par 66.

King's Acre

One of 1997's new arrivals, created by Graham Webster from Aberdeenshire and given two years to mature before golf was allowed. This lovely layout could be one of the great success stories of new course development. Situated just outside the city boundary at Lasswade "pay-as-you-play" at £15 per round and a super test of all aspects of your golfing abilities.
5,666 yards, par 70.

Kingsknowe

Good golf course, good clubhouse, friendly and welcoming membership and maintaining a reputation for high quality of course presentation. For city visitors, a lovely course for a day's golf.
5,979 yards, par 69.

Prestonfield: The well protected 2nd green is framed by laburnum and overlooked by the familiar bulk of Arthur's Seat.

Torphin Hill: Panoramic views of Edinburgh from the top of the course, this one featuring the clubhouse and par 3 first hole.

King's Acre: Glorious summer sunshine lights up the big bunker protecting the right hand side of the 18th green.

Kingsknowe: Looking down on the 11th Green from the backdrop of fir trees of this downhill par 3.

Turnhouse

Situated close to Edinburgh Airport, Turnhouse was in excellent condition in 1997 and remains one of the city's best loved venues. The top of the course can be windy but the varied eighteen holes demand versatility and accuracy. Superb clubhouse hospitality is guaranteed! 6,121 yards, par 70.

Turnhouse: Ladies' medal day at this popular west Edinburgh club. The green at the par 3, eleventh (106 yds) is well protected!

Buchanan Castle

Home course of the legendary Eric Brown and situated in glorious parkland west of Drymen. One of the finest clubhouses in Strathclyde. 5,668 yards, par 68.

Helensburgh

A stiff inward half needs energy and accuracy; looks down on the Firth of Clyde and makes use of lovely trees, burns and the slopes of the hillside above the town. A superb clubhouse completes the scene. 5,773 yards, par 69.

Loch Lomond

Scotland's newest entrant to the world championship of "Best Courses". A wonderful experience, designed brilliantly by Tom Weiskopf, where his creative golfing imagination has married perfectly with the natural habitat. Fairways like greens, greens like snooker tables - it is in astonishing condition. No room for faint hearts or lack of experience of the big course.
6,730 yards, par 72.

Buchanan Castle: "Duncan Cameron's lochan" - the 8th - is all about club selection and accuracy; par 3, 137 yards.

Helensburgh: One of the best par 3's in Strathclyde; the 11th is 172 yards (downhill, ditch & bunkers) - and a great view!

Loch Lomond: A great finishing hole for Scotland's newest contribution to World Championship golf; 415 yards, par 4.

West Kilbride

One of the Ayrshire coast's most under-rated courses - and there are more than a few. Situated alongside the Firth of Clyde, where the prevailing south westerlies can easily wreck a round, with the 383 yard thirteenth adjacent to the beach, one of the classic par 4's in Scotland. Great golf, great views and a superbly appointed clubhouse.
6,452 yards, par 71.

Turnberry

1995 Open venue, scene of many a dramatic finish; beautiful links golf on both the Ailsa and Arran courses. This is an extremely searching location where all aspects of your game will be severely tested but it is a lovely experience - the hotel which overlooks the scene is a legend in itself.
Ailsa - 6,950 yards, par 70.
Arran - 6,276 yards, par 69.
(P.S: Greg Norman reduced the Ailsa course to 63!?).

West Kilbride: Looking back from the rear of the well guarded 4th green; 163 yards, par 3.

Turnberry: The grandeur of the hotel is ever available; here it is the backdrop to a view from above the 5th green.

Cowal: The short 5th; total carry from tee to elevated sloping green; almost an impossible 3 if you mishit the tee shot.

Rothesay: Looking to Arran and the "Sleeping Warrior" from the back of the par 4, 7th green (307 yards).

Cowal

Beautifully created in the hillside north of Dunoon, this is arguably the stiffest course on the western seaboard (Ayrshire excepted!) Some absolutely superb holes (the dog leg fourth is something else) where resident pro Russell Weir remains one of the most popular in Scotland. A brand new clubhouse awaits after your round.
5,791 yards, par 69.

Rothesay

One of Scotland's traditional - and most enjoyed - holiday courses. Situated around Canada Hill, with a 360 degree panorama from the top of the course. Not long, but some climbs and wind can complicate things. Guaranteed warm welcome from Jim Dougal in the pro shop - and the members in the clubhouse.
5,395 yards par 69.

Port Bannatyne

Relaxing golf at its best here, with nothing above 316 yards to test you. Thirteen holes (plus the first five again) add a bit of spice but it is the scenery which steals the show.
4,506 yards, par 68.

STRATHCLYDE - Port Bannatyne: Spectacular views abound, but this one over the 1st green towards Cowal is one of the best.

Brechin: Perfect conditions for golf in Angus; Brechin's 14th green affords great views north to the glens.

Brechin

Now split by the main Aberdeen trunk road, the parkland of this fine eighteen holes offers excellent golf. A particularly interesting back nine where four opportunities from ten to thirteen to pick up a birdie are swiftly followed by three where bogeys are likely! A lovely setting in typical Angus countryside.
5,634 yards, par 69.

Alyth

Another super Angus course with a lovely layout spread over the countryside east of the town. Trees and rolling fairways make accuracy off the tee important and this is another venue where the inward nine is at least two shots harder than the outward. Tom Melville is the genial resident Professional and a terrific clubhouse awaits after the day's sport.
5,943 yards, par 70.

Alyth: Ladies medal day; a putt for par on the 155 yard third (sorry - 135 yards from the ladies tee!)

Pitlochry

Set on the rising ground between Moulin and fir-covered Craigower Hill, this is another of Perthshire's lovely holiday courses. A fair climb over the first few holes but enjoyment all the way on a very well tended layout. The traditional clubhouse, now modernised inside, is warm and welcoming.
5,811 yards, par 69.

Aberfeldy

Now extended to eighteen holes, the little course at Aberfeldy is tailor made for the holiday golfer. The shorter inward half offers up several opportunities to produce a flattering score but it needs approach work and putting at its best to achieve that.
5,014 yards, par 68.

Pitlochry: The view down the 18th towards the green and clubhouse, but the autumn rowan steals the show!

Aberfeldy: the view back down the 1st towards the town, with the short 18th and the clubhouse prominent.

Downfield

Under-rated by many and under-utilised for tournaments, this surely is one of Scotland's finest and most difficult courses of championship standard. A wonderful design amidst glorious tree lined fairways it is hard to believe the course is in the middle of Dundee. Open Qualifier, not for the faint hearted and a major achievement if you complete your round to handicap.

6,266 yards, par 70.

Rosemount

It is unfair to single out one golf course from an area of the country which offers so much quality but Rosemount's claim to be the best inland course north of the Tay is understandable. Wonderful layout, tight for driving, requiring an accurate short game and its immaculate presentation (the greens were in fabulous shape on my visit) makes it a joy to play. The second course (The Lansdowne) - is also splendid and but a couple of strokes shorter.

6,378 yards, par 71.

Downfield: Just one of the many superb holes on the course; the approach to the 11th must carry the pond __and__ ditch!

Rosemount: The short (121 yards) 15th; club choice crucial and accuracy essential to avoid sand.

Edzell

This little town boasts one of Angus' best courses - and there are more than a few! Great use of the natural features, plenty hazards (natural and man made) and a superb clubhouse; resident Professional Alistair Webster is one of the best on the "Tartan Tour".
6,348 yards, par 71.

Edzell: Not yet daybreak; a lovely view back down the 1st towards the clubhouse before play begins.

Monifieth

One of the Open Qualifying courses, these are splendid links which at their eastern end almost link up to another - the Panmure Club at Barry. A really stiff test on typical seaside terrain with tight fairways compounding the natural heughs and howes of the links.
6,459 yards, par 71.

Monifieth: One of the most wickedly placed bunkers on the course, beside the 16th green - "Wilderness".

Strathtay

A "hidden gem" of a holiday golf course at Grandtully, close to the river Tay between Aberfeldy and Pitlochry. Some steep climbs, really tight fairways, but glorious Perthshire scenery all around. A course for short irons, for pure enjoyment and for relaxation - nowhere else could breaking a course record be of less significance.
5,283 yards, par 68.

Strathtay: Bluebells everywhere around this lovely little course.
Through the trees the green of the dog-leg 3rd is featured.

THE DEFINITIVE 1998
Golf in Scotland

SUPPLEMENT TO APPEAR ALONGSIDE

February issue
(on sale 18th January 1998)

Europe's Best Selling Golf Magazine
Sales 84,293 *(ABC Jan-June 1997)*

TODAY'S GOLFER

March issue
(on sale 1st February 1998)

Read by Fanatical, Upmarket Golfers
Sales 65,055 *(ABC Jan-June 1997)*

The 48-page supplement will devote 75% of the contents to editorial promoting golfing holidays in Scotland.

This will embrace price comparisons from budget holidays to the aspirational, covering golf courses that range from the famous and well known to highlighting some of the best of the new courses.

For further information please telephone 0171-817 9649

emap.
PURSUIT PUBLISHING LTD

Where to stay

As much as the golf courses of Scotland provide the opportunity for the visitor to enjoy the sport at its best, no holiday can be enjoyed to the full unless a careful selection of accommodation is made. Our 'Where to Stay' section provides an enormous choice of facilities to suit every budget and taste. Scottish landlords and landladies are famed for their hospitality and friendliness. As you will see many of them can provide complete packages which simplify the planning of a sporting holiday. We are sure you will find in this section of the guide, the key to a wonderful visit to Scotland.

Inver Hotel
Crathie
Aberdeenshire AB35 5UL
Tel/Fax: (013397) 42345

The hotel is located at the west end of the village of Crathie and is one and a half miles from Balmoral castle, the Highland home of Her Majesty the Queen. All rooms are en-suite with T.V. and tea/coffee making facilities. The hotel is on the Deeside Road which has the Grampian and Cairngorm Mountains as a stunning backdrop. Leisure pursuits for visitors include golf, fishing, deer-stalking, walking, mountaineering and skiing.
The Inver is a family-run hotel, privately owned by Dave and Jenny Whinnet. There is a Lounge Bar with a warm and friendly atmosphere where guests can all meet and quickly get to know each other, not to mention partaking of the selection of Malt Whiskies which Dave, your Mine Host will serve and gladly give some background information.

HOTEL SEAFORTH
DUNDEE ROAD, ARBROATH DD11 1QF

Only a short drive from Carnoustie and within easy range of many fine courses, the Seaforth is an ideal base for the golfer. And what more could you want at the 19th hole than good food - fine steaks and fish, including our famous 'Smokies' - good cheer in our comfortable bar and an indoor pool and jacuzzi to soak away the sorrow of missing the green at the 13th. 20 en-suite bedrooms with tea/coffee making facilities, telephone and colour television.

Tel: (01241) 872232   Fax: (01241) 877473

AA ★ ★   **RAC** ★ ★

Managed by the same family for over 30 years, the well established Station Hotel has recently been refurbished to a very high standard. Ideally located, it is conveniently close to a wide selection of shops, sandy beach and the world famous Championship Golf Course.

All our bedrooms, many wth sea views, have en-suite facilities, are equipped with colour TV, hospitality trays and full central heating. For your safety a current fire certificate is held.

Our hotel is renowned for good food. Traditional Scottish meals are temptingly served with ample portions.Home made soups and steak pie are established favourites and fresh-locally caught-fish dishes are served daily in either of our popular bars or attractive dining-room.

Station Hotel
CARNOUSTIE

Station Road, Carnoustie, Angus, Scotland DD7 6AR   Tel: (01241) 852447

The Rosely Country House Hotel

14 EN-SUITE BEDROOMS

A beautiful Victorian, listed Baronial residence, surrounded by 4 acres of woodlands and secluded gardens, on the edge of rural Angus. Good food and friendly service are hallmarks of this family run hotel. Within comfortable driving distance are some of the world's most famous golf courses. If however your passion is for hillwalking, fishing, shooting or sightseeing, the Rosely is conveniently situated to pursue all these interests.

Carnoustie	10 mins
Downfield	20 mins
St. Andrews	40 mins
Monifeith	15 mins
Barry	15 mins
Edzell	20 mins
Blairgowrie	45 mins
Letham Grange	5 mins
Panmure	15 mins
Forfar	15 mins
Brechin	15 mins

For additional information & brochure:
Contact: The Rosely Country House Hotel, Arbroath, Angus,
DD11 3RD. Tel: 012418 76828. Fax: 012418 76828

CARLOGIE HOUSE HOTEL

All bedrooms have en-suite facilities, with ground floor courtyard bedrooms suitable for the disabled.

A la carte restaurant, lounge bar, lunch & supper meals available

Carlogie House Hotel,
Carlogie Road,
Carnoustie,
Angus DD7 6LD.
Tel: (01241) 853185

LETHAM GRANGE RESORT

In the heartland of golf lies the superb Letham Grange Hotel and Golf Courses. The magnificent Victorian Mansion nestles within the panoramic countryside. The Mansion has been restored to its former glory as a top quality hotel offering a style which is both traditional and sumptuous.

36 holes of magnificent golf! Widely acclaimed as one of the premier courses in Scotland, the Old Course provides a blend of tree lined parkland and open rolling fairways. With water playing a major role, the course is both scenic and dramatic. The New Course, although slightly shorter - and without the water hazards - offers golfers a more relaxed and less arduous round. However, it can be deceptive!

For further information on special golfing breaks or a day's golf please contact:
Letham Grange Hotel, Colliston, by Arbroath DD11 4RL.
Tel: (01241) 890373. Fax: (01241) 890414.

Scottish Tourist Board
HIGHLY COMMENDED
●●●●

Resipole Golf Course

A really stunning location, on the Ardmanurchan peninsula, Resipole Golf Course lies between the mountains and the shore line of Loch Sunart. On the north side of the Loch this newest of the West Highland golf courses is just 28 miles west of Fort William, on the A861 between Salen and Strontian.

This magnificent nine hole 1900 yd course has all the demanding facets you would expect from a well planned course. Only in its first season, it has all the natural hazards, perfectly balanced, that will give it the reputation that all golfers enjoy - a challenge! A must for all visitors as well as local golfers.

There are excellent restaurant and bar facilities available both for snacks or a delicious evening meal with a wine list second to none. Resipole Farm offers self catering accommodation and a five star touring park. Be assured of a friendly welcome at this truly splendid location on the shores of Loch Sunart.

Contact Tel: (01967) 431235 Fax: (01967) 431777

THE MACHRIE HOTEL & GOLF LINKS

Port Ellen, Isle of Islay, Argyll PA42 7AN Tel: (01496) 302310 Fax: (01496) 302404

Originally built as a farmhouse 250 years ago, the Machrie provides 16 en-suite bedrooms within the hotel, 6 to a superior standard. There are also 15 twin bedroom fully furnished lodges available for self catering or golfing packages. First class cuisine using fresh local produce and a warm and friendly service provide the perfect place to stay. With a challenging 18 hole par 70 traditional links course adjacent to the hotel, it is the ideal location for those who want the luxury of a unique course on the doorstep.

ABBOTSFORD HOTEL
CORSEHILL ROAD, AYR
RECOMMENDED FOR GOLFERS

En-suite facilities, T.V., tea maker, olde worlde atmosphere, secluded garden. Winter rates October/March. Special party rates.
Restaurant facilities and bar meals available. For further details contact:

ALLAN A.R. HUNTER
Resident Proprietor
Tel/Fax: (01292) 261506

BELLEISLE HOUSE HOTEL
Open Jan-Dec

Belleisle House Hotel is set in the heart of Burns country, the immediate surrounds include two fine parkland golf courses, an aviary, a deer park and many beautiful walks. What better atmosphere in which to prepare oneself for any important meeting, or plot a coup at Ayr Races, or just take a well earned rest. Those who prefer it can take one of the many walks in the grounds and should not miss the celebrated gardens. Belleisle House is only 2 miles from the centre of Ayr, 5 miles from Prestwick Airport, 2 miles from Ayr Racecourse and less than 1 mile from Ayr's sandy beaches.

For further details, contact:
Belleisle House Hotel,
Belleisle Park,
Ayr KA7 4DU.
Tel: (01292) 442331
Fax: (01292) 445325

BELLEISLE AND SEAFIELD COURSES
Belleisle Park, Ayr
Tel: (01292) 441258

18th green, Belleisle.

A fair proportion of golfing pilgrims to the Ayrshire coast may unadvisedly bypass the many public courses on offer, including *Belleisle* and *Seafield*. *Belleisle* is far from a course of modest aspiration, designed simply to satisfy an increasingly insatiable demand for the game.

A great deal of re-styling and development of the *Seafield* golf course has taken place in recent years. Its opening hole is short, some 218 yards played from an elevated tee, over the Curtecan Burn. This hole is some indication of the quality now of *Belleisle's* sister course and the first tees of both courses are only 200 yards apart with the finishing greens side by side.

Southfield Hotel

An elegant Georgian house quietly located in its own grounds convenient to town centre, beach, bowling greens, tennis courts, golf courses (5 miles from Turnberry). 40 cover restaurant. Lounge bar. Open all day. Food all day. Open to non-residents. Children welcome. All bedrooms en-suite. Group and weekly discounts available. Douglas, Jean, Craig and all the staff guarantee a homely welcome and comfortable stay.

**Southfield Hotel, The Avenue, Girvan KA26 9DS.
Tel: (01465) 714222.
Fax: (01465) 712405.**

Priory House Hotel

The Priory stands within 6 acres of delightful landscaped and secret gardens. Savour the grand elevated promenade position with outstanding scenery and breathtaking sunsets. Four poster beds, jacuzzi's, coal fires make this an idyllic setting for any occasion. Superb cuisine by our award winning chef is served in the breathtaking Four Seasons Restaurant or The Conservatory Restaurant.

**Broomfield, Largs,
Ayrshire KA30 8DR .
Tel: (01475) 686460   Fax: 01475 689070**

Manor Park Hotel

*Manor Park Hotel was built at the turn of the 1900's. It is situated in a rural location, surrounded by scenic countryside, but minutes from Prestwick Airport, Scotland's gateway to America and other international and UK destinations. With 12 individually furnished rooms, Conservatory and Courtyard Function Suite, its warm welcome extends itself to the most intimate occasion or wedding celebration. Golf enthusiasts may take advantage of some of Scotland's most famous golf courses which are just minutes drive from Manor Park. Conference and business facilities are available.
I would have great pleasure in welcoming you to the Manor Park Hotel.
CHARLES PRICE - MANAGING DIRECTOR*

HOTEL & RESTAURANT *48 Kilmarnock Road, Monkton, Ayrshire KA9 2RJ Tel/Fax: (01292) 479365*

RAC ACCLAIMED

Kincaig Private Hotel

AA RECOMMENDED

**39 AYR ROAD, PRESTWICK, AYRSHIRE KA9 1SY
Telephone/Fax: (01292) 479480**

A family run hotel in the heart of Scotland's golfing paradise. On the Ayr/Prestwick road convenient for town centre, airport and railway station. Comfortable en suite rooms, CTV, radio, teamaking facilities. Residents licence. Lounge with Video/TV. Car parking. Ideally situated for Northfield Bowling Complex and Prestwick Indoor, Centrum and Ayr racecourse.

LOCKERBIE GOLF CLUB
Corrie Road,
Lockerbie DG11 2ND

This is an 18 hole parkland course in an open agricultural setting with delightful views of the surrounding countryside. The course was extended in 1986 from 9 holes to 18 and now provides a very reasonable challenge for golfers of all abilities.
There is a modern clubhouse with changing and shower facilities for both ladies and gents. Bar and catering facilities are available during the season (April-October).
There are no restrictions on visitor play during the week. Handicap certificates are not required.

For further information, please contact the secretary, JIM THOMSON on (01576) 203363

THE CRAIGDARROCH ARMS HOTEL
High Street, Moniaive, Thornhill,
Dumfriesshire DG3 4HN
Tel: (01848) 200205

A warm friendly welcome awaits golfers and fishers in our family run hotel. The Craigdarroch Arms Hotel is situated in a friendly unspoilt picturesque village which has connections with James Renwick, one of the last Covenanters and Annie Laurie, who was born at nearby Maxwelton House. There is golfing and fishing within short travelling distances, and our hotel offers well stocked bars, en-suite bedrooms and a wide selection of homemade food served in our Macara's Restaurant.
Please contact Moira, Kenny or Sheena.

REDLANDS
COUNTRY LODGE
BY LADYBANK, FIFE KY15 7SH.
FAX/TELEPHONE: (01337) 831091.
JIM & DOROTHY McGREGOR

A converted gamekeepers' cottage, plus a Norwegian pine lodge with four en-suite bedrooms, each with a colour TV, tea/coffee facilities and central heating, and with a comfortable guests' lounge. Meals are taken in the adjacent cottage.

An ideal base for touring and golf, with 25 courses within 20 miles, and only half a mile from Ladybank with its main line station.

Redlands is a non smoking house, and we pride ourselves on our warm friendly welcome, and our excellent home cooking.

GOLF CLUB & HOTEL

In a delightful setting, just 8 miles from St. Andrews and 4 miles from Dundee, Drumoig is a fabulous new Golf Resort Hotel (4 Crowns Highly Commended) ideally situated to explore the picturesque East Neuk of Fife, and the highlands of Tayside & Perthshire.

Set amidst its own 18 hole championship golf course, and close to many of Scotland's most historic courses, Drumoig has 24 bedrooms all with Satellite TV, Tea/Coffee Tray and Trouser Press, some rooms also have balconies overlooking the 18th fairway.

● Pay & Play from £12 per round

● Superb Clubhouse with restaurant & bar overlooking 18th green and private lochs

● Golf Breaks including 2 night Dinner, Bed & Breakfast from £99

DRUMOIG GOLF CLUB & HOTEL
Drumoig, Leuchars, St Andrews, Fife KY16 0BE
Tel: (01382) 541800 Fax: (01382) 542211
email: drumoig@standrews.co.uk

The Sporting Laird Hotel & Apartments

St. Andrews

* SMALL PRIVATE LICENSED HOTEL.
* CENTRALLY LOCATED IN ST. ANDREWS BETWEEN GOLF COURSES AND SHOPS.
* GOLF PACKAGES AND GOLF BREAKS AVAILABLE.
* KATE'S RESTAURANT: EXCELLENT CUISINE
* BARGAIN BREAKS FOR THE NON-GOLFER.
* GROUP AND WEEKLY DISCOUNTS AVAILABLE.
* 200 YARDS FROM OLD COURSE.
     ALL ROOMS EN-SUITE

Also available-luxury West Sands Apartments-overlooking St. Andrews Bay and other

FOR FULL COLOUR BROCHURE APPLY TO:
THE SPORTING LAIRD HOTEL &
APARTMENTS,
5 PLAYFAIR TERRACE, ST. ANDREWS,
FIFE,
SCOTLAND KY16 9HX.
TEL: (01334) 475906. FAX: (01334) 473881.
EMAIL : SLAIRDSCO@AOL.COM
WWB: HTTP: WWW.STANDREWS.CO.UK/HOTELS/LAIRD/LAIRD.HTM

Scottish Tourist Board
COMMENDED

The Russell Hotel

Situated on The Scores overlooking St.Andrews Bay, this small friendly hotel personally run by Gordon and Fiona de Vries offers you good food and comfortable accommodation. It is 2 mins. walk from 1st tee of the Old Course and just as convenient for the town centre and beaches. The hotel has ten twin/double rooms all with en suite facilities with Satellite TV. It is fully licensed and the restaurant is always busy at weekends and during the summer months making reservations necessary.

The Russell has developed a fine reputation for excellent cuisine and exceptional service. Golf parties welcome

The Scores, St. Andrews,
Fife KY16 9AS
Tel: (01334) 473447
Fax: (01334) 478279

Yorkston House

68/70 Argyle Street,
St. Andrews, Fife KY16 9BU
Telephone/Fax: (01334) 472019

Comfortable guest house close to town centre. Central heating throughout.
All bedrooms have washbasin, alarm clock, hairdryer, colour TV and tea/coffee making facilities. Most rooms en-suite.
Late key provided. Breakfast from 7.30 am if required.
Telephone, fax or write for further details.

THE SANDFORD COUNTRY HOUSE HOTEL

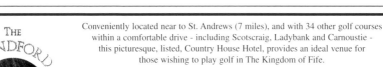

Conveniently located near to St. Andrews (7 miles), and with 34 other golf courses within a comfortable drive - including Scotscraig, Ladybank and Carnoustie - this picturesque, listed, Country House Hotel, provides an ideal venue for those wishing to play golf in The Kingdom of Fife.

Set in seven acres of private grounds, the 16 en-suite bedroom Sandford Hotel, is renowned for its traditional style and warm, friendly service. Fine Scottish and European cuisine is the hallmark of Head Chef Steven Johnstone.

STB *Highly Commended, member of 'A Taste of Scotland' and 'Where to Eat in Scotland'*

THE SANDFORD COUNTRY HOUSE HOTEL, Newton Hill, Wormit,
near Dundee, The Kingdom of Fife, Scotland DD6 8RG.
Telephone: (01382) 541802   Fax: (01382) 542136

Ayr: Seafield

Galloway for your 1998 Holiday

High-quality self-catering accommodation.
About 200 houses throughout South West Scotland.

❊ Peaceful Country Cottages   ❊ Elegant Country Houses
❊ Convenient Town Houses   ❊ Quiet Farm Houses

SUPERB SCENERY, SANDY BEACHES, FRIENDLY PEOPLE,
EXCELLENT GOLF COURSES

For free colour brochure, contact: G. M. THOMSON & CO.,
27 King Street, Castle Douglas, Kirkcudbrightshire DG7 1AB.
Tel: (01556) 504030 (24hr. answering service).
Fax: (01556) 503277.

Dumfries & Galloway

 ★ ★   ★ ★

IMPERIAL HOTEL, CASTLE DOUGLAS, KIRKCUDBRIGHTSHIRE

THE IMPERIAL HOTEL
35 KING STREET, CASTLE DOUGLAS
TEL: (01556) 502086
"GOLFING GREATS"

Ideally situated in the centre of Dumfries and Galloway, just a short "Drive"
away is the championship Links at Southerness, 2 x 18 at Dumfries,
Kirkcudbright, Glenluce, Stranraer plus a variety of testing 9 hole courses for
the higher handicapper. The golfing proprietor will reserve your tee off times
and arrange your golf itinerary - see the golf photos in the "Golfing Hotel".
Dinner, Bed & Full Scottish Breakfast in en-suite rooms with tea/coffee,
colour TVs & telephone from £34.50 p.p. for a minimum 2 day stay. Late bar,
drying facilities, club storage.
A WARM WELCOME AWAITS
SEND FOR BROCHURE & GOLF INFORMATION

Clonyard House Hotel   AA ★★   RAC ★★★★

COLVEND, DALBEATTIE, KIRKCUDBRIGHTSHIRE
Ashley Courtenay,

The ideal centre for your golfing holiday. 4 golf courses within 10 miles
including Southerness Championship Course.
After an exhilarating (or frustrating) day on the golf course, relax in the
warm and friendly surroundings of this country hotel. All rooms ensuite
with lashings of hot water to soak away the aches and pains of the day. A
superb meal, a bottle of good wine, convivial company in the bar, what
more can one want?

Telephone: Nick Thompson on (01556) 630372

DOUGLAS ARMS HOTEL

King Street, Castle Douglas, Kirkcudbrightshire DG7 1DB
Tel: (01556) 502231 Fax: (01556) 504000

Scottish Tourist Board
COMMENDED

Centrally situated in the heart of Dumfies and Galloway, the Douglas Arms
Hotel is the perfect choice for your golfing holiday. The hotel is central to a
wide variety of superb golf courses, Kirkcudbright, Southerness & Colvend
for a start. After a hard day on the fairways and greens, relax in our cosy
lounge bar and restaurant and enjoy some delicious food and drink. We have
secure undercover parking for our guests. For further information please call
on the above number.

92

Murrayfield golf course

NUMBER THIRTY SIX

36 St. Vincent Crescent, Glasgow G3 8NG.
Tel/Fax: 0141-248 2086
Mobile: 0585 562382

S.T.B. Listed Commended

Number Thirty Six is a Victorian House situated on the edge of Glasgow City Centre close to the West End. We are just a stones throw away from the S.E.C.C., the Art Galleries and Museum and some of the best restaurants, pubs and shops in Glasgow. Our bedrooms are tastefully and individually decorated with all rooms having private facilities. Room rates include a continental breakfast served in the comfort and privacy of your own room.

TARIFF
SINGLES £25-£35
TWINS/DOUBLES £46-£60

HOLLY HOUSE

S.T.B. Listed Commended

Holly House is a mid terrace Early Victorian building standing in a tree lined terrace with ample car parking in the city centre South area. Local places of interest being Burrell Gallery, Rennie Mackintosh Art Lovers House, Ibrox Football Stadium. The SECC, airport and city centre are all within 5-10 minutes whilst the Ibrox Underground is just around the corner. The accommodation is set out as singles, twins, doubles and a few large family rooms all well appointed with central heating, colour TV's etc. Being privately owned, you are assured a warm welcome awaits you.

Room rates to include breakfast:
Singles £20-£30
Twins/Doubles £36-£60
Family £60-£70

Contact: Peter N. Divers,

Holly House,

54 Ibrox Terrace,

Glasgow G51 2TB.

Tel: 0141-427 5609. Fax: 0141-427 5608. Mobile: 0850 223500.
"Member of The Harry James Appreciation Society"

KIRKLAND HOUSE
42 ST. VINCENT Crescent,
GLASGOW G3 8NG

S.T.B. Listed Commended

City Centre guest house located in Glasgow's little Chelsea, a beautiful Victorian Crescent in the area known as Finnieston offers excellent rooms most with en-suite facilities, full central heating, colour TV, tea/coffee makers. The house is located within walking distance of Scottish Exhibition Centre, Museum-Art Gallery and Kelvingrove Park. We are very convenient to all City centre and West End facilities also only ten minutes from Glasgow's International Airport. Our house is featured in the Frommers Tour Guide and we are also Scottish Tourist Board Listed Commended. St. Vincent Crescent runs parallel with Argyle Street and Sauchiehall Street in the central Kelvingrove area near to Kelvingrove Park and Art Gallery Museum.

ROOM RATES
Singles £25-£35 Twins/Doubles £50-£70
TEL: 0141-248 3458 FAX: 0141 - 221 5174
MOBILE NUMBER 0385 924282
Members of the "Harry James Appreciation Society".
Ask for details.

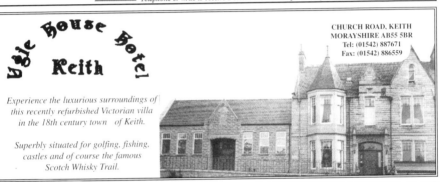

ALTON BURN ROAD
NAIRN
HIGHLAND IV12 5ND
TEL: (01667) 452051

Situated in its own ground well away from the main thoroughfare lies the Alton Burn Hotel managed and run by the MacDonald family since 1956. The hotel has a warm and friendly atmosphere. There are 25 bedrooms all with private bathrooms, colour TV, radio, baby listening and welcome tray. Our spacious dining room is well known for its excellent cuisine and varied menus. Recreation facilities abound and one can have a relaxing round on the putting green or an exacting game of tennis. We also have an outdoor heated swimming pool.

Nairn has two championship courses as well as one nine hole course. We can arrange tee times and golfing breaks for you or your party. Not forgetting that in 1999 Nairn is the host to The Walker Cup - so book your accommodation now.

For further information contact:
MRS J. MACDONALD, ALTON BURN HOTEL, NAIRN TEL: (01667) 453325/452051

" The Claymore." Quality hospitality through attention to detail.

Recently fully refurbished the Claymore House Hotel is pleased to offer you the warmest of welcomes.

Situated in a quiet residential area close to the beach, and between two championship golf courses, it has something for everyone.

The bar with the open fire for the cooler evenings, provides an excellent meeting place for that early evening aperitif, right through to the after dinner whisky. The wine list is extensive but moderately priced, complementing the excellent traditional and continental cuisine, created from the finest Scottish local produce.

The rooms are all en-suited with baths or showers and incorporate, direct dial telephones, remote control colour television, hair dryers, and tea and coffee making facilities.

Whatever your reason for staying in Nairn, the Claymore House Hotel has something for you. Sporting breaks, business breaks, family holidays, highland touring holidays... or just a few days away from it all, you can rest assured by staying at the Claymore. When you're looking for more - choose the Claymore.

With over 25 golf courses within one hour to suit all standards and budgets Nairn is without doubt the capital of Golf's Northern Mecca.
Choose from:- Royal Dornoch, Nairn Dunbar, Nairn (Hosts to Walker Cup 1999), Moray Old or Boat of Garten, all within easy reach.

The Claymore House Hotel
Seabank Road, Nairn, Scotland. IV12 4EY
Telephone: 01667-453731
Facsimile: 01667-455290

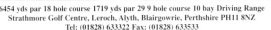

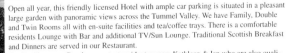

"Summer at Skibo"
by Alan Grant
GOLF SECRETARY

Summer like the swallow comes
Without fail every year
It brings lots of our members
From around the world to here.

The "here" I mean is Skibo
A place that's more than dreams
The fairyland of peace it's called
How appropriate this seems

Let's start off with the building
it's both large and grandiose
A repisit'ry of history
From Carnegie to Montrose

The rooms are grand and varied
From palatial to the cosy
The heating system guarantees
Your cheeks are always rosy.

Amusement is provided by
activities galore
Be careful when horse riding
It can make your bottom sore.

But then the girls down at the spa
Can deal with the malaise
With oils and rubs they banish pain
In aromatic ways.

And then it's time for dinner
In the splendid dining room
Wine glasses just like fish tanks
Guarantee there is no gloom

Ascend to your bedroom
Like a condor on the wing
It's hard not to believe
That you can hear the angels sing

So take all these ingredients
Which our club has clearly got
And stir them all together
In a great big melting pot

Surprise will greet the outcome
And bring pleasure to our hearts
This club is surely greater
Than the total of its parts

So, continue with your visits
Come as often as you're able
Together we'll escape into
This highland castle fable.

The Bardman, May 1997

108

TWENTY FOUR GOLF COURSES
within an hour.
To include Taymouth Castle, Crieff, Auchterarder and King James the 6th on Moncrieffe Island. Privately run Hotel in spectacular lochside setting. Well placed in Central Scotland for many day trips. Excellent choice of walking, fishing and watersports. Lochview Restaurant serving the finest Scottish cuisine, and an extensive choice of good value bar meals. Friendly service in a relaxed atmosphere.

● GOLF BREAKS ●

The Nines - includes FIVE Days of free Golf from £275.00 (excl. Sat).
The Eighteens - includes THREE Day tickets - choice of five local courses from £310 (weekdays only).
Golf Breaks include six nights Dinner, Bed and Breakfast.

TAILOR MADE GOLF BREAKS.
GROUP/SOCIETY DISCOUNT

**Please contact Andrew Low
CLACHAN COTTAGE HOTEL,
(Dept ScotGol)
Lochearnhead, Perthshire FK19 8PU
Scotland.
Tel: (01567) 830247 Fax: (01567) 830300**

RAC ★★

Scottish Tourist Board
COMMENDED
♛♛♛

The Old Course, St. Andrews

GOLF COURSES WITHIN AN HOUR'S DRIVE
COURTESY VEHICLES
DISCOUNT PRIVILEGE WITH MOST COURSES

CLUBS WELCOME

Special 3 day breaks

CLUBS FOR HIRE

Packed Lunches

Bar Snacks Supper Room Acclaimed Restaurant

HALF AN HOUR FROM FERRIES TO IRELAND

A small family run hotel with adjacent luxury log cabin which can be used as self catering accomodation. A friendly bar that never closes! (subject to the license) No juke box and no fruit machines. Probably the best food in the South West of Scotland.

40 acres of grounds to walk in, with fishing for trout and coarse fish in the hotel pools. free tuition is available. Clay pigeon shooting, said to be the best shooting layout in Scotland.

Novices welcome, professional instruction is available.

Full board from £27.50 - £55.00 per day, per person

Self catering from £9.00 - £15.00 per day, per person

For further details contact:
TORWOOD HOUSE COUNTRY SPORTING HOTEL
GASS BY THREE LOCHS
WIGTOWNSHIRE DG8 0PB
Tel/Fax: (01581) 300 469

Great UK Courses Become More Accessible

Improving your game by playing as many courses as possible has, until now, been costly in both time and money. A solution has been offered by Airkilroe, the air charter company, that will expand the choice of courses available and allow players a round or two further away from home.

Their new scheme can fly a party to the course of their choice, timed for their convenience. It can avoid the cost of an overnight stay and playing at far-flung courses can now be an easily affordable daytrip. Each trip is tailor-made for the party and can fit any schedule proposed making this luxury service the easiest way to play where and when you want.

Although Airkilroe originally set the scheme up for business and promotional golfing days, demand grew from private groups. "This scheme broadens the choice of courses for players. It makes the courses in Ireland, Scotland, the Southwest and even parts of the Continent available to many more. Players can choose their course and times, have the most luxurious trip *and* save money says Brian Hetherington of Airkilroe.
Contact Airkilroe on: 0161-436 2055.

The changing face of Scottish Golf

East Lothian is home to many of the world's finest golf courses, most of which were created during the golf course development boom of 100 years ago. These courses have their own style and traditions which reflect to a great extent, their Victorian origins.

A new kind of course, however is being developed today which meets the needs and lifestyle of the 1990s golfer. One of the most outstanding of these is at Whitekirk, between North Berwick and the A1. This 18-hole par 71 course is a golf academy, run by the Director of Golf, Chris Patey who is himself an experienced teacher. This caters for individuals or groups, beginners or scratch players.

Moreover, you do not need to rush straight out on to the course and loosen up your swing over the first few holes. There is a 300 yard long practice range for warming up or simply just working on your game.

The clubhouse too is at your disposal. As you would expect its magnificent

Whitekirk: 5th green

loses nothing in its architecture to its long established neighbours. In fact, it is set in breathtaking scenery with a backdrop dominated by the imposing shape of the Bass Rock.

The much abused expression "user friendly" describes Whitekirk very well. Everyone is welcome. The green fees are realistic at around £15 on weekdays and £20 at the weekends. Families are encouraged, ladies hold coffee mornings, there are collective lessons and demonstrations as regular features on the calendar. In fact, here

lounge looks out over the Bass Rock as well as the golf course. The restaurant is so good it attracts local non golfers. All in all, Whitekirk, while representing all the good traditions of a great East Lothian golf course, offers to every golfer, aspiring or experienced, the facilities of the future.

For more information contact:
Chris Patey, Director of Golf,
Whitekirk Golf Course,
nr. North Berwick,
East Lothian EH42 1XS.
Tel: (01620) 870300.

ABERDEENSHIRE

Aberdeen

* Auchmill Golf Course
Aberdeen City Council,
Arts & Recreation Dept.,
St. Nicholas House,
Broad Street,
Aberdeen AB10 1GU.
Tel: (01224) 522000.
18 holes, length of course
5082 yds.
Charges: On Application.
Starter: (01224) 714577.

Balgownie Golf Course
Royal Aberdeen Golf Club
(2 courses),
Balgownie, Bridge of Don,
Aberdeen AB23 8AT.
Tel: (01224) 702571 (clubhouse).
Balgownie Links - 18 holes,
length of course 6372 yds.
Par 70
Silverburn Links - 18 holes,
length of course 4066 yds.
Par 60
Charges: Balgownie -
Weekdays, £40 per round, £60
daily.
Silverburn - Weekdays, £20 per
round,
£30 daily.
For advance reservations
Tel: (01224) 702221.
A practice area and full
catering facilities are available.
Visitors welcome - weekend
restrictions. Letter of
introduction required.
Secretary: Mr. Fraser Webster -
Tel: (01224) 702571.
Professional: Mr. Ronnie
MacAskill -
Tel: (01224) 702221.

* Balnagask Golf Club
Aberdeen City Council,
Arts & Recreation Dept.,
St. Nicholas House,
Broad Street,
Aberdeen AB10 1GU.
Tel: (01224) 522000.
18 holes, length of course
5472 yds.
Charges: On Application.
Starter: (01224) 876407.

* Bon Accord Golf Club
19 Golf Road,
Aberdeen AB24 5QB.
Tel: (01224) 633464.
18 holes, length of course
6270 yds.
SSS 69
Charges: telephone
Aberdeen Leisure on
(01224) 647647.
Visitors are welcome.
Catering facilities available.
Secretary: C. Wheeler -
Tel: (01224) 633464.

Caledonian Golf Club
20 Golf Road,
Aberdeen AB24 5QB.
Tel: (01224) 632443.
18 holes, length of course
6437 yds.
SSS 69
Charges: £7.30 round.
For advance reservations
Tel: (01224) 632269.
6 hole course nearby.
Charges: £2.50 (round).
Catering facilities are available.
Entertainment Friday/Saturday
Evenings.
Visitors most welcome.
Secretary: John A. Bridgeford -
Tel: (01224) 632443.

Deeside Golf Club
Bieldside,
Aberdeen AB1 9DL.
Tel: (01224) 869457.
18 holes, length of course
5971 yds.
SSS 69
Charges: £25 per day;
£30 weekends/bank holidays.
A practice area, caddy cars
and catering facilities are
available.
Visitors are welcome
Mon-Fri and Sun.
Professional: Frank Coutts -
Tel: (01224) 861041.

* Hazlehead Golf Course
Aberdeen City Council,
Arts & Recreation Dept.,
St. Nicholas House,
Broad Street,
Aberdeen AB10 1GU.
Tel: (01224) 522000.
2 x 18 hole courses.

Lengths 5673m, 5303m.
9 hole course, length 2531m
Charges: On Application.
Starter: (01224) 321830.
Professional: Mr. I. Smith -
Tel: (01224) 317336.

* Kings Links Golf Course
Aberdeen City Council,
Arts & Recreation Dept.,
St. Nicholas House,
Broad Street,
Aberdeen AB10 1GU.
Tel: (01224) 522000.
6 holes, length of course
5731 yds.
Charges: On Application.
Starter: (01224) 632269.
Professional: Mr. B. Davidson -
Tel: (01224) 641577.

Murcar Golf Club
Bridge of Don,
Aberdeen AB23 8BD.
Tel: (01224) 704345.
18 holes, length of course
6240 yds.
SSS 71
Charges: £28 round, £38 daily.
For advance reservations
Tel: (01224) 704354/704370.
Caddy cars and catering
facilities are available.
Visitors are welcome all week
except Sats/Suns before noon
and Wed afternoons.
Secretary: D. Corstorphine -
Tel: (01224) 704354.

Peterculter Golf Club
Burnside Road,
Peterculter, Aberdeen.
Tel: (01224) 735245.
18 holes, length of course
5601 yds.
SSS 69
Charges: £11 round, £16 daily.
For advance reservations
Tel: 901224) 734994.
Practice area, caddy cars and
catering facilities available.
Visitors welcome at all times.
Secretary: K. Anderson -
Tel: (01224) 735245.
Professional: D. Vannet -
Tel: (01224) 724994.

Rosehearty Golf Club
Aberdeen AB43 4JP.
Tel: (01346) 571250.
9 holes, length of course
4018m/4397 yds.
SSS 62
Charges: £5 Mon-Fri round, £7
weekend round. £8 Mon-Fri
daily, £10 weekend daily.
For advance reservations
Tel: (01346) 571250.
Catering facilities available and
visitors welcome all week.
Secretary: A. Downie -
Tel: (01346) 571477.

Westhill Golf Club (1977)
Westhill Heights,
Westhill,
Aberdeenshire AB32 6RY.
Tel: (01224) 742567.
18 holes, length of course
5849 yds.
SSS 69
Charges: On Application.
For advance reservations
Tel: (01224) 740159.
Caddy cars, practice area and
catering facilities are available.
Visitors are welcome all week
except Sat and Mon-Fri 4.00-
7.00pm.
Administrator - Amelia Burt
Tel: (01224) 742567.
Professional: R. McDonald -
Tel: (01224) 740159.

Aboyne

Aboyne Golf Club
Formaston Park, Aboyne.
Tel: (01339) 886328.
18 holes, length of course
5910 yds.
SSS 68
Charges: On Application.
For advance reservations
Tel: (01339) 887078 (Sec).
A practice area, caddy cars and
catering facilities are available.
Visitors are welcome all week.
Secretary: Mrs. Mairi MacLean -
Tel: (01339) 887078.
Professional: I. Wright.

Alford

Alford Golf Club,
Montgarrie Road,
Alford.
Tel: (019755) 62178.
18 holes, length of course
5402 yds.
SSS 65
Charges: Mon-Fri - £12,
weekend- £19 per round.
Mon-Fri - £17,
weekend - £24 daily.
For advance reservations Tel:
(019755) 62178.
A practice area and catering
facilities are available.
Visitors are welcome all week.
Please check for weekends.
Club Secretary: Bob Fiddes -
Tel: (019755) 62178.

Ballater

Ballater Golf Club
Victoria Road,
Ballater AB35 5QX.
Tel: (01339) 755567.
18 holes, length of course
5638 yds.
Par 67
Charges: On application.
For advance reservations Tel:
(01339) 755567/755658.
A practice area, caddy cars and
catering facilities are available.
Visitors are welcome Monday
to Friday.
Secretary: A. Barclay -
Tel: (01339) 755567.
Professional: F. Smith -
Tel: (01339) 755658.
Caterer: Mrs. M. Todd -
Tel: (01339) 756241.

Braemar

Braemar Golf Course
Cluniebank Road,
Braemar.
Tel: (01339) 741618.
18 holes, length of course
4916 yds.
SSS 64
Charges: On Application.
For advance reservations Tel:

(01339) 741618.
Caddy cars and catering
facilities are available.
Visitors are welcome all week.
Secretary: John Pennet -
Tel: (01224) 704471.

Cruden Bay

Cruden Bay Golf Club
Aulton Road, Cruden Bay.
Tel: (01779) 812285.
18 and 9 holes, length of
course 5848m/6395 yds.
SSS 72 (18), 65 (9)
Charges: On application
For advance reservations
Tel: (01779) 812285.
A practice area, caddy cars
and catering facilities are
available.
Visitors are welcome all week
but restricted at weekends. No
society bookings at weekends.
Administration: R. Pittendrigh -
Tel: (01779) 812285.
Professional: Robbie Stewart -
Tel: (01779) 812414.

Ellon

McDonald Golf Club
Hospital Road, Ellon.
Tel: (01358) 720576.
18 holes.
SSS 69
Charges: On Application.
Catering facilities available on
request
Secretary: George Ironside -
Tel: (01358) 720576.
Professional: Ronnie
Urquhart - Tel: (01358)
722891.
Fax: (01358) 720001.

Fraserburgh

Fraserburgh Golf Club
Philorth, Fraserburgh.
Tel: (01346) 518287.
18 holes, length of course
6279 yds.
SSS 70
9 holes, length of course
3400 yds.
Charges: £17 daily (Mon-Fri),

£22 (Sat/Sun). £50 weekly.
A practice area and catering
facilities are available.
Secretary: Mr. A.D. Stewart -Tel:
901346) 516616.

Huntly

Huntly Golf Club
Cooper Park,
Huntly AB54 4SH.
Tel: 901466) 792643.
18 holes, length of course
5399 yds.
SSS 66
Charges: £13 (weekdays), £20
(weekends) daily.
Catering facilities are
available.

Insch

Insch Golf Club
Golf Terrace,
Insch AB5 6JY.
Tel: (01464) 820363
9 holes, length of course:
men's 5,632 yds,
ladies 4,972 yds.
SSS 67 mens
SSS 69 ladies
Charges: On Application.
For advance reservations Tel:
(01464) 820291.
Tees reserved on Mondays
from 4.30pm (Ladies);
Tuesdays from 5pm (Gents);
Wednesdays from 4.30pm
(Juniors).
Visitors are welcome at any
other time.
Secretary: B. Leith -
Tel: (01464) 820144.

Inverallochy

*Inverallochy Golf Course
Inverallochy,
nr. Fraserburgh.
Tel: (01346) 582000.
18 holes, length of course
5137 yds.
Par 64.
(Further details on
application).

Inverurie

Inverurie Golf Club
Davah Wood,
Blackhall Road,
Inverurie AB51 5JB.
Tel: (01467) 620207/620193.
18 holes, length of course
5711 yds.
SSS 68
Charges: £18 (Mon-Fri),
£24 (Sat/Sun) daily.
Catering
facilities are available.
Wide wheeled caddy cars only.

Kemnay

Kemnay Golf Club
Monymusk Road,
Kemnay.
Tel: (01467) 642060.
18 holes, length of course 5903
yds.
SSS 69
Charges: Weekdays £16 round,
£20 daily. Weekends £18 round,
£22 daily.
For advance reservations Tel:
(01467) 642225.
Full catering and bar
facilities available.
Visitors welcome: Telephone for
starting times.
Administrator: - George Berstan
Tel: (01467) 643746.

Kintore

Kintore Golf Club
Balbithan Road, Kintore.
Tel: (01467) 632631.
18 holes, length of course
5997 yds.
SSS 69
Charges: £11 midweek per
round,
£16 weekends.
For advance reservations Tel:
(01467) 632631.
Visitors are welcome all week
except between 4pm-7pm
Mon, Wed and Fri Apr-Sept.
Secretary: Mrs. Vicki Graham.

Newburgh-on-Ythan

**Newburgh-on-Ythan
Golf Club**
26 Elder Road,Newburgh, Ellon
AB41 6FD.
Tel: (01358) 789436.
18 holes, length of course
6162 yds.
SSS 70
Charges: £13 daily (weekdays)
£18 daily, (weekends).
For advance reservations Tel:
(01358) 789058 (Clubhouse).
A practice area is available.
Visitors are welcome all week
but club competitions every
Tuesday evening.Catering
available by arrangement.
Secretary: Mr. E. Leslie.
Tel: (01358)789436.

Newmachar

Newmachar Golf Club
Swailend,Newmachar
AB21 7UU.
Tel: (01651) 863002.
Fax: (01651) 863055.
Hawkshill Course - 18 holes,
length of course
6623 yds.
SSS 74
Charges: £20 round, £30 day
(Mon-Fri), £30 round, £45 day
(Sat/Sun).
Swailend Course - 18 holes,
length of course 6388 yds.
SSS 70.
Charges: £15 round, £25 day
(Mon-Fri). £25 round, £35 day
(Sat/Sun).
One round on each course £27
(Mon-Fri) £45 (Sat/Sun).
For advance reservations Tel:
(01651) 863002. Driving Range,
practice bunker and chipping
area, putting green. Powered
buggies and caddy cars for hire.
Fully licensed clubhouse with
catering available 7 days.
Visitors welcome (advance
booking recommended).
Secretary/Manager:
George A. McIntosh.
Tel: (01651) 863002.
Director of Golf: Peter Smith.
Tel/Fax: (01651) 863222.

Old Meldrum

Old Meldrum Golf Club
Kirk Brae, Old Meldrum.
Tel: (01651) 872648.
18 holes, length of course
5988 yards.
SSS 69 (Par 70) Medal Tees
SSS 66 (Par 68) Forward Tees
Charges: Per round/daily - £12
Mon-Fri, £18 Sat/Sun, weekly
(Mon-Fri) £40.
For reservations Tel: Pro shop -
(0651) 873555.
Visitors and visiting parties
welcome.
A practice area and bar facilities
are available.
Secretary: D.Petrie -
Tel: (0651) 872383.
Professional: John Caven.

Peterhead

Peterhead Golf Club
Craigewan Links, Riverside
Drive,
Peterhead AB42 1LT..
Tel: (01779) 472149.
Old Course: 18 holes, length
of course 6173 yds.
SSS 71
Charges: £16 round/£22 daily
weekdays. £20 round/£27 daily
weekends.
No Society outings Saturdays.
New Course: 9 holes, length
of course 2237 yds.
Charges: £9 round/daily.
Juniors £4.
A practice area and limited
catering facilities are
available.
Visitors are welcome all week
- restricted on Saturdays.
Secretary: Tel: (01779) 472149.
Fax: (01779) 480725.

Portlethen

Portlethen Golf Club
Badentoy Road,
Portlethen AB12 4YA.
Tel: (01224) 781090.
Fax: (01224) 781090.
18 holes, length of course
6707 yds.
SSS 72

Charges: £14 weekdays,
£21 weekends/Bank holidays per
round.
£21 weekdays (only) daily.
For advance reservations Tel:
(01224) 781090.
Caddy cars, practice area and
catering facilities are
available.
Visitors are welcome Mon-Fri;
weekend with member.
Secretary: Mr. B.F. Mole.
Tel: (01224) 781090.
Professional: Muriel Thomson -
Tel/Fax: (01224) 782571.

Tarland

Tarland Golf Club
Aberdeen Road, Tarland.
Tel: (01339) 881413.
9 holes, length of course
5386m/5888 yds.
SSS 68 (18 holes)
Charges: £11 Mon-Fri. £13
Sat/Sun (1995).
For advance reservations Tel:
(01339) 881413.
Caddy cars and practice area
are available.
Visitors are welcome all week,
but 'phone for weekends.
Secretary: R.G. Reid.
Tel: (013398) 81413 (Apr-Oct).
(013398) 81571 (Oct-Apr).

Turriff

Turriff Golf Club
Rosehall, Turriff.
Tel: (01888) 562982.
18 holes, length of course
6107 yds.
SSS 69
Charges: On Application.
For advance reservations Tel:
(01888) 563025.
Small practice area, clubs,
caddy cars and catering
facilities are available.
Visitors are welcome all week
and after 10am Sat/Sun.
Hon Secretary: Mr. Bert Greig -
Tel: (01888) 562982.
Professional: Mr. R. Smith -
Tel: (01888) 563025.

ANGUS

Arbroath

*Arbroath Golf Course
Arbroath Artisan Golf Club
(Playing over above)
Elliot, by Arbroath.
Tel: (01241) 872069.
18 holes, length of course
6185 yds.
SSS 70
Charges: £15 round (Mon-Fri),
£20 round (Sat/Sun). £20 daily
(Mon-Fri), £30 daily (Sat/Sun).
For advance reservations Tel:
(01241) 875837.
A practice area, caddy cars, hire
clubs and catering facilities are
available.
Visitors are welcome all week.
Secretary: J. Knox -
Tel: (01241) 876131.
Professional: J. Lindsay Ewart -
Tel: (01241) 875837.

Letham Grange Golf Club
Colliston,
by Arbroath DD11 4RL.
Tel: (01241) 890373.
Old Course - 18 holes, length of
course: Blue - 6968yds; White -
6632 yds; Yellow - 6348 yds; Red
5774 yds.
SSS 73
Charges: £21 round, £32 daily
(Mon-Fri). £32 round (Sat/Sun
and public holidays).
New Course - 18 holes, length of
course: White - 5528 yds; Yellow
- 5276 yds; Red - 4687 yds.
SSS 68
Charges: £13 per round, £19
daily
(Mon-Fri). £16 round, £26 daily
(Sat/Sun
and public holidays).
1 round on each course - £27
weekdays; £42 weekends.
Practice areas (putting/chip-
ping/bunker), powered
buggies and catering facilities
available.
Visitors are welcome all week.
Secretary: Hotel -
Tel: (01241) 890373.
Professional: Golf Desk -
Tel: (01241) 890377.

Barry

Panmure Golf Club
Burnside Road, Barry,
by Carnoustie DD7 7RT.
Tel: (01241) 853120.
18 holes, length of course
6317 yds.
SSS 71
Charges: On application.
For advance reservations
Tel: (01241) 855120.
A practice area, caddy cars and
catering facilities are available.
Visitors are welcome all week,
except Saturdays.
Secretary;
Major (ret'd) G.W. Paton -
Tel: (01241) 855120.
Professional: Neil Mackintosh -
Tel: (01241) 852460.

Brechin

Brechin Golf and Squash Club
Trinity,
by Brechin DD9 7PD.
Tel: (01356) 622383.
18 holes, length of course
6096 yds.
SSS 70
Charges: On application.
Catering facilities available.
Visitors are welcome without
reservation.
Secretary: A.B. May -
Tel: (01356) 622326.
Professional: S. Rennie -
Tel: (01356) 625270.

Carnoustie

Carnoustie Golf Links
*Buddon Links Course
Links Parade,
Carnoustie DD7 7JE.
18 holes, length of course
5420 yds.
SSS 66
Charges: £14 round, Juniors
(14-18) £7, Juvenile
(under 14)round 50p. Day ticket
£21.
For advance reservations Tel:
(01241) 853789.
Caddies, caddy cars and
catering facilities are

available.
Visitors are welcome all week.
Secretary: Mr. E.J.C. Smith.

Carnoustie Golf Links
*Burnside Course
Links Parade,
Carnoustie DD7 7JB.
18 holes, length of course
6020 yds.
SSS 69
Charges: £18 round, Juniors
(14-18) £9, Juvenile
round (under 14) £4. Day ticket
£27.
For advance reservations Tel:
(01241) 853789.
Caddies, caddy cars (no caddy
cars Nov-Apr incl.) and
catering facilities are
available.
Visitors are welcome all week.
Secretary: Mr. E.J.C. Smith.

Caledonia Golf Club
Links Parade.
Tel: (01241) 852115.
Clubhouse facilties are avail-
able.
Membership Fees: £15 per year.
(Further details on
application).

Carnoustie Golf Club
3 Links Parade.
Tel: (01241) 852480.
Secretary D.W. Curtis -
Tel: (01241) 852480.
(Further details on application.)

*Carnoustie Golf Links
Championship Course
Links Parade,
Carnoustie DD7 7JE.
18 holes, length of course
6936 yds.
SSS 75
Charges: £36 round.
Day ticket £63.
For advance reservations Tel:
(01241) 853789.
Caddies, caddy cars (no caddy
cars Nov-Apr incl) and
catering facilities are
available.
Visitors are welcome all week,
except Saturday morning and
before 11.30am Sunday.
Secretary: Mr. E.J.C. Smith.

Dalhousie Golf Club
Links Parade,
Carnoustie.
(Further details on
application).

Mercantile Golf Club
c/o The Secretary,
Police House, Dunlappie Road,
Edzell, Angus DD9 7UB.
Tel: (01356) 648222 (Office).
(01356) 647304 (Home). Email:
Dougal191@aol.com
Secretary: Douglas Ogilvie.
(further details on
application).

*New Taymouth Golf Club
Taymouth Street,
Carnoustie.
Tel: (01241) 852425.
(further details on
application).

Dundee

*Camperdown Golf Course
Camperdown Park, Dundee.
Tel: (01382) 623398.
Visitors contact: Art &
Recreation Division, Tayside
House, Dundee.
Tel: (01382) 434000 (ext. 2872).
Secretary: K. McCreery Tel -
(01382) 642925.
(Further details on
application).

Downfield Golf Club
Turnberry Avenue, Dundee.
Tel: (01382) 825595.
Fax: (01382) 813111.
18 holes, length of course
6822 yds
SSS 73
Charges: £30 round, £45 daily
£35 per round (weekends).
Caddies, caddy cars, practice
area and catering facilities
available.
Visitors are welcome
weekdays and Sunday pm -
parties welcome with
pre-booking essential. Other
times-Saturday and Sunday
call starter on day of play after
8.00am.
Secretary: Barrie D. Liddle -
Tel: (01382) 825595.

Professional/Starter:
Kenny Hutton -
Tel: (01382) 889246.

Edzell

The Edzell Golf Club
High Street,
Edzell DD9 7TF.
Tel: (01356) 648235
(clubhouse)
18 holes, length of course
6348 yds.
SSS 71
Charges: Weekday £20 round,
weekend £26 round. Weekday
£30 daily, weekend £39 daily.
£90 weekly - excluding Sat &
Sun.
For advance reservations
Tel: (01356) 647283.
A practice area, caddy cars and
catering facilities are available
(caddies by arrangement).
Visitors are welcome all week.
Secretary: I. Farquhar -
Tel: (01356) 647283.
Professional: A.J. Webster -
Tel: (01356) 648462.
Driving Range - 300 yds -
opened in 1997.
Visitors Welcome.

Forfar

Forfar Golf Club
Cunninghill, Arbroath Road,
Forfar DD8 2RL.
Tel: (01307) 462120.
18 holes, length of course
6052 yds.
SSS 70
Charges: £16 round
(Mon-Fri), £24 daily.
Sat/Sun £32 daily, £20 per
round.
For advance reservations Tel:
(01307) 463773.
Fax: (01307) 468495.
A practice area, caddy cars
and catering facilities are
available.
Visitors are welcome all week.
Managing Secretary: W. Baird -
Tel: (01307) 463773.
Professional: Mr. P. McNiven -
Tel: (01307) 465683.

Kirriemuir

Kirriemuir Golf Club
Northmuir, Kirriemuir.
Tel: (01575) 572144.
18 holes, length of course
5553 yds.
SSS 67
Charges: On Application.
Practice area, caddy cars and
catering facilities are
available.
Visitors are welcome
weekdays.
Professional: Mr. Anthony Caira
Tel: (01575) 573317.
Fax: (01575) 574608.

Monifieth

Ashludie Golf Course
The Links, Monifieth.
Tel: (01382) 532967.
18 holes, length of course
5123 yds.
SSS 66
Charges: On Application.
For party reservations Tel:
(01382) 535553.
Caddy cars and catering
facilities are available.
Visitors are welcome Monday
to Friday after 9.30am.
Saturday after 2pm and
Sundays after 10am.
Secretary: H.R. Nicoll -
Tel: (01382) 535553.
Professional: Ian McLeod -
Tel: (01382) 532945.

Broughty Golf Club
6 Princes Street,
Monifieth, Dundee.
Tel: (01382) 532147.
For advance reservations Tel:
(01382) 532767.
A practice area, caddy cars
and catering facilities are
available.
Visitors are welcome all week
and after 2pm on Saturdays.
Secretary: A. Allardice -
Tel: (01382) 532147
Professional: Ian McLeod -
Tel: (01382) 532945.

Medal Course
The Links, Monifieth.
Tel: (01382) 532767.
18 holes, length of course
6657 yds.
SSS 72
Charges: On Application.
For party reservations Tel:
(01382) 535553.
Caddy cars and catering
facilities are available.
Visitors are welcome Monday
to Friday after 9.30am.
Saturday after 2pm and
Sunday after 10am.
Secretary: H.R. Nicoll -
Tel: (01382) 535553.
Professional: Ian McLeod -
Tel: (01382) 532945.

Montrose

Mercantile Golf Club
East Links, Montrose DD10
8SW..
Tel: (01674) 672408
Secretary: D.D. Scott -
Tel: (01674) 675716.
(Further details on
application)

*Montrose Links Trust
Traill Drive,
Montrose DD10 8SW.
Tel: (01674) 672932.
Fax: (01674) 671800.
Medal- 18 holes, length of
course 6470 yds.
Broomfield - 18 holes, length
of course 4765 yds.
SSS 72
SSS 63
Charges: Medal- Mon-Fri £30
daily, £42 Sat & Sun. Mon-Fri
£20 round, £28 Sat & Sun.
Weekly £95 adult, £48 junior.
Broomfield- Mon-Fri
£10 round, £14 Sat & Sun.
Weekly £60 adult, £30 junior.
Reductions for juniors,
members' guests and
unemployed.
For advance reservations Tel:
(01674) 672932.
Caddy cars, practice area and
catering facilities are
available.
Visitors are welcome all week

No visitors on Saturdays.
Visitors allowed Sundays after
10am on Medal Course.
Secretary: Mrs. Margaret
Stewart -
Tel: (01674) 672932.
Professional: Kevin Stables -
Tel (01674) 672634.

ARGYLL
Blairmore

Blairmore & Strone Golf Club
High Road, Blairmore,
by Dunoon PA23 8JJ.
Tel: (01369) 840676.
9 (18) holes, length of course
1933m/2112 yds.
Charges: On Application.
Vistors are welcome all week,
except Saturday afternoon.
Secretary: J.C. Fleming -
Tel: (01369) 860307.

Isle of Colonsay Golf Club
Machrens Farm, Isle of
Colonsay PA61 7YP.
Tel: (01951) 200364.
18 holes, length of course
4475 yds.
SSS 73
Charges: Annual membership £5
Caddie cars available and visitors welcome at all times.
Secretary: Hugh McNeil -
Tel: (01951) 200364.

Campbeltown

The Machrihanish Golf Club
Machrihanish,
by Campbeltown.
Tel: (01586) 810213.
18 and 9 holes, length of course
6228 yds.
SSS 71
Charges: Sun-Fri £21 (18), £10
(9) round. £30 (18), £10 (9)
daily (Mon-Fri). Weekly £120
(18), £40 (9), £36 day Sat.
Sat Day Ticket only £30
(18), £10 (9), Children 14
years and under - half price on
the 9 hole course.
For advance reservations Tel:
(01586) 810277.
A practice area, caddy cars

and catering facilities are
available.
Visitors are welcome all week
Secretary: Mrs. A. Anderson -
Tel: (01586) 810213.
Professional: Mr. K. Campbell -
Tel: (01586) 810277.

Carradale

Carradale Golf Course
Carradale, Kintyre.
Tel: (01583) 431643.
9 holes, length of course
2387 yds.
SSS 64
Charges: £8 daily, £40 weekly.
For advance reservations Tel:
(01583) 431643.
Visitors welcome all week.
Secretary: J. R. Ogilvie -
Tel: (01583) 431643.

Dalmally

Dalmally Golf Club
Dalmally PA33 1AS.
9 holes.
SSS 63
Charges: £10 daily.
Visitors are welcome.
Secretary: A.J. Burke.
For Information:
Tel: (01838) 200370.

Dunoon

Cowal Golf Club
Ardenslate Road, Dunoon.
Tel/Fax: (01369) 705673.
18 holes, length of course
6063 yds.
SSS 70
Charges: £16 round
(Mon-Fri); £24 round
(Sat/Sun), £75 week ticket
(weekdays).
For advance reservations
Tel/Fax:
(01369) 705673.
Caddy cars and catering
facilities are available.
Secretary: Wilma Fraser -
Tel/Fax: (01369) 705673
Professional Russell .D. Weir.

Innellan

Innellan Golf Club
Innellan.
Tel: (01369) 703242.
9 holes, length of course
18 holes 4246m/4642 yds.
SSS 64
Charges: £10 day.
Catering facilities are
available.
Visitors are welcome all week,
except Mon, from 5pm.
Secretary: A. Wilson -
Tel: (01369) 702573.

Inveraray

Inveraray Golf Club,
A83 - Lochgilphead Road,
Inveraray.
Tel: (01499) 302508.
9 holes, length of course
5600 yards (18).
SSS 68
Charges: Adults weekdays and
weekends - £10 per day.
Visitors very welcome.
Various facilities nearby.
Capt: David Wilkinson.

Lochgilphead

Lochgilphead Golf Club
Blarbuie Road, Lochgilphead.
Tel: (01546) 602340.
9 holes, length of course
4484 yds.
SSS 63
Visitors welcome. Licensed.
Clubhouse available. Open competitions in summer.
Secretary: N. McKay -
Tel: (01546) 603840 (after 6pm).

Oban

Glencruitten Golf Course
Glencruitten Road, Oban.
Tel: (01631) 562868.
18 holes, length of course
4452 yds.
SSS 63
Charges: On Application.
For advance reservations Tel:
(01631) 62868.
A practice area and catering

facilities are available. Visitors are welcome Tues, Wed, Fri and Sun.
Secretary: A.G. Brown -
Tel: (01631) 564604
(after 6 pm).

Southend

Dunaverty Golf Club
Southend,
by Campeltown.
Tel: (01586) 830677.
18 holes, length of course
4799 yds.
SSS 64
Charges: On Application.
For advance reservations
Tel: (01586) 830698/677.
Visitors are welcome all week
without reservation, but check
for club competitions.
Secretary: David S. Ure -
Tel: (01586) 830684.

Tarbert
Kilberry Road, Tarbert.
Tel: (01880) 820565.
9 holes, length of course
4744 yds.
SSS 64
Charges: On Application.
Licensed clubhouse available.
Visitors are welcome without
reservation.
Secretary: Peter Cupples -
Tel: (01880) 820536.

Taynuilt

Taynuilt Golf Club
Laroch, Taynuilt PA35 1JE.
9 holes, length of course
4302 yds.
SSS Gents 61, Ladies 64
Charges: On Application.
Visitors are welcome all week.
Secretary: Murray Sim-
Tel: (01866) 822429.

Tighnabruaich

Kyles of Bute Golf Club
The Moss, Kames,
Tighnabruaich PA21 2EE.
9 holes, length of course
2389 yds.

SSS 64
Charges: £8 per week day. £10
Saturday and Sunday.
Secretary: Dr. J. Thomson -
Tel: (01700) 811603.

AYRSHIRE
Ayr

*Belleisle Golf Course
Belleisle Park, Ayr.
c/o South Ayrshire Council,
Burns House, Burns Statue
Square,
Ayr KA7 1UT.
Tel: (01292) 441258.
18 holes, length of course
64 yds
SSS 6431
Charges: £17 round, £24 daily,
£80 weekly (Mon-Fri). (1996)
For advance reservations Tel:
(01292) 441258.
A practice area, caddy cars and
catering facilities are available.
Visitors are welcome all week.
Starters Office -
Tel: (01292) 441258.
Professional: Mr. D. Gemmell -
Tel: (01292) 441314.

***Dalmilling Municipal Golf
Club**
Westwood Avenue, Ayr.
c/o South Ayrshire Council,
Burns House, Burns Statue
Square,
Ayr KA7 1UT.
Tel: (01292) 263893.
18 holes, length of course
5724 yds.
SSS 68
Charges: £11 round, £18 daily,
£80 weekly (Mon-Fri). (1996)
For advance reservations
Tel: (01292) 263893.
Caddy cars, practice area and
catering facilities are available.
Visitors are welcome all week.
Starters Office -
Tel: (01292) 263893.
Professional: Philip Cheyney
Tel: (01292) 263893.

*Seafield Golf Course
Belleisle Park, Ayr.
c/o South Ayrshire Council,
Burns House, Burns Statue

Square,
Ayr KA7 1UT.
Tel: (01292) 441258.
18 holes, length of course
5481
SSS 67
Charges: £11 round, £18 daily,
£80 weekly (Mon-Fri). (1996)
For advance reservations
Tel: (01292) 441258.
Practice area, caddy cars and
catering facilities available.
Visitors welcome all week.
Starters Office -
Tel: (01292) 441258.
Professional: David Gemmell -
Tel: (01292) 441314.

Barassie

**Kilmarnock (Barassie) Golf
Club**
29 Hillhouse Road,
Barassie, Troon KA10 6SY.
Tel: (01292) 313920.
27 holes, length of course
5896m/6450 yds. 18 holes 6484,
9 holes 2756
SSS 73
Charges:18 holes £32.50, 27
holes £40, 36 holes £50. For
advance reservations Tel:
(01292) 313920.
A practice area, caddy cars
and catering facilities are
available.
Visitors are welcome
Mon/Tues/Thur/Fri pm.
Secretary: R.L. Bryce -
Tel: (01292) 313920
Professional: Tel: (01292)
311322.

Beith

Beith Golf Club
Bigholm Road,
Beith KA15 2YQ.
Tel: (01505) 503166.
(Further details on
application).

Gailes

Glasgow Golf Club
Gailes, Irvine.
Tel: (01294) 311258.
18 holes, length of course

5954 m/6513 yds.
SSS 72
Charges: £42 round Mon-Fri,
£52 daily.
Sat & Sun pm only £47 (1998)
Deposit £10 per person
required.
For advance reservations
Tel: 0141 - 942 2011.
Fax: 0141 - 942 0770.
A practice area, caddy cars and
catering facilities are available.
Caddies available by prior
arrangement.
Professional: Mr. J. Steven -
Tel: (01294) 311561.

Western Gailes Golf Club
Gailes, Irvine KA11 5AE.
Tel: (01294) 311649.
18 holes, length of course
6639 yds.
SSS 73
Charges: £50 round, £75 daily.
For advance reservations
Tel: (01294) 311649.
Caddies, caddy cars and cater-
ing facilities available.
Visitors welcome Mon, Tues,
Wed and Fri.
Secretary: Andrew McBean -
Tel: (01294) 311649.

Galston
Loudoun Golf Club
Galston KA4 8PA.
Tel: (01563) 821993.
(Further details on
application).

Girvan
Brunston Castle Golf Club,
Dailly, by Girvan.
Tel: (01465) 811471.
18 holes, length of course
6792 yds.
SSS 72
Charges: Mon-Fri £22.50 per
round,
weekends £27.50 per round.
Daily- £30 Mon-Fri, weekends
£35.
For advance reservations Tel:
(01465) 811471.
Caddy cars/motor buggies,
practice area and catering
facilities are available.
Visitors are welcome all week.

Secretary: Ian F. Tennant.

*Girvan Golf Club
Golf Course Road, Girvan.
c/o South Ayrshire Council,
Burns House, Burns Statue
Square,
Ayr KA7 1UT.
Tel: (01465) 714346.
18 holes, length of course
5064 yds.
SSS 64
Charges: £11 round, £18 daily,
£80 weekly (Mon-Fri). (1996)
Trolleys are available.
Practice area, caddy cars and
catering facilities available.
Visitors welcome all week.
Starters Office -
Tel: (01465) 714346.
Professional: David Gemmell -
Tel: (01292) 441314.

Irvine
The Irvine Golf Club
Bogside, Irvine.
Tel: (01294) 275979.
18 holes, length of course
5858m/6408 yds.
SSS 71
Charges: On Application.
For advance reservations Tel:
(01294) 75979.
A practice area, caddy cars
and catering facilities are
available (caddies by
arrangement).
Visitors are welcome by
arrangement.
Secretary: Mr. Andrew
Morton - Tel: (01294) 275979.
Professional: Mr. Keith
Erskine - Tel: (01294) 275626.

*Ravenspark Golf Course
13 Kidsneuk, Irvine.
Tel: (01294) 271293.
18 holes, length of course 6543
yds.
SSS 71
Charges: £8.40 round Mon-Fri,
£14.10 day Mon-Fri, £12.50
round Sat-Sun, £19 day Sat-
Sun.
Visitors welcome except before
2.30pm on Sat. from March -
Oct.

Full catering and bar facilities.
Secretary: G. Robertson -
Tel: (01294) 554617.
Professional: P. Bond -
Tel: (01294) 276467.
Steward: J. McVey -
Tel: (01294) 271293.

Kilbirnie
Kilbirnie Place Golf Club
Largs Road, Kilbirnie.
Tel: (01505) 683398.
18 holes, length of course
5500 yds.
SSS 67
Charges: On Application.
Catering facilities are
available.
Visitors are welcome, except
Saturdays.
Secretary: J.C. Walker -
Tel: (01505) 683283.

Kilmarnock
Annanhill Golf Club
Irvine Road, Kilmarnock
KA1 2RT.
Tel: (01563) 521644.
18 holes, length of course
6269 yds.
SSS 70
Charges: £9.50 Mon-Fri. £18
Daily. Saturday, Sundays and
Bank Holidays £18 Daily.
For advance reservations
Tel: (01563) 521644.
Practice area available and
catering facilities by
arrangement.
Visitors welcome all week
except Saturdays.
Secretary: Mr. Thomas
Denham-
Tel: (01563) 521644.

*Caprington Golf Club
Ayr Road, Kilmarnock.
Tel: (01563) 521915.
(Further details on
application).

Largs
Largs Golf Club
Irvine Road,
Largs KA30 8EU.
Tel: (01475) 673594.

18 holes, length of course
6237 yds.
SSS 71
Charges: £25 round, £35 daily.
For advance reservations
Tel/Fax:
(01475) 673594.
A practice area, caddy cars and
catering facilities are
available.
Visitors are welcome all week.
Parties - Tues & Thurs.
Secretary: D. McGillivray -
Tel/Fax:(01475) 67354.
Professional: R. Collinson -
Tel: (01475) 686192.

Routenburn Golf Club
Routenburn Road, Largs.
Tel: (01475) 673230.
18 holes, length of course
5604 yds.
SSS 68
Charges: £7.30 Mon-Fri, £12
Sat/Sun round. £12.20 Mon-Fri,
£18.20 Sat/Sun daily.
For advance reservations
Tel: (01475) 687240.
Practice area, caddy cars and
catering facilities available.
Visitors welcome.
Secretary: Mr. Joe Thomson -
Tel: (01475) 675755.
Professional: Mr. G. McQueen -
Tel: (01475) 687240.

Mauchline

Ballochmyle Golf Club
Mauchline KA5 6LE.
Tel: (01290) 550469.
Fax: (01290) 553150.
18 holes, length of course
5990 yds.
SSS 69
Charges: On application.
Catering facilities are
available.
Visitors are welcome with
reservation.
Secretary: D.G. Munro -
Tel: (01290) 550469.

Maybole
*Maybole Golf Course
Memorial Park, Maybole.
c/o South Ayrshire Council,
Burns House, Burns Statue

Square,
Ayr KA7 1UT.
Tel: (01292) 612000.
9 holes, length of course
2635 yds.
SSS 33
Charges: £7 round, £11 daily,
£80 weekly (Mon-Fri).
For advance reservations
Tel: (01292) 263893.
Caddy cars available.
Visitors welcome all week.
Booking Officer -
Tel: (01292) 612000.
Professional: Pillip Cheyney -
Tel: (01292) 263893.

Muirkirk

Muirkirk Golf Club,
Furnace Road, Muirkirk.
9 holes, length of course
5350m (18 holes).
SSS 66
Charges: On Application.
For advance reservations Tel:
(01290) 661257.
A practice area and catering
facilities are available.
Visitors are welcome all week.
Secretary:
Mrs. M. Cassagranda -
Tel: (01290) 661556.

New Cumnock

New Cumnock Golf Club
Lochill, Cumnock Road,
New Cumnock KA18 4BQ.
Tel: (01290) 338848.
9 holes, length of course
5176 yds (18).
SSS 66
Charges: £8 daily.
Catering facilities weekends
only.
Visitors welcome all times
except Sunday mornings and
afternoons
(competition times).
Secretary: Dickson Scott.

Patna

Doon Valley Golf Club
Hillside, Patna KA6 7JT.
Tel: (01292) 531607.
9 holes, length of course

5152 yds
SSS Medal 69
Yellow Trees 66
Charges: £8 round, £15 daily.
For advance reservations
Tel: (01292) 531607.
Visitors welcome weekdays,
weekends by arrangement.
Secretary: H F Johnstone MBE-
Tel: (01292) 550411.

Prestwick

Prestwick Golf Club
2 Links Road, Prestwick.
Tel: (01292) 477404.
18 holes, length of course
6544 yds.
SSS 73
Charges: On application.
Caddies, caddy cars, practice
area and catering facilities are
available.
Visitors are welcome Mon,
Wed & Fri 8.00-8.50 am,
10.10 am-12.30 pm and 2.40-
4.00pm.
Thursday 8.00-11.30 am. No vis-
itors at weekends or on a
Thursday afternoon.
Secretary: I.T. Bunch.
Professional: F.C. Rennie.

Prestwick
St. Cuthbert Golf Club
East Road,
Prestwick KA9 2SX.
Tel: (01292) 477101.
18 holes, length of course
6470 yds.
SSS 71
Charges: £20 round, £27 daily.
For advance reservations Tel:
(01292) 477101.
Catering facilities (except
Thursdays) are available.
Visitors are welcome Monday
to Friday (not on weekends or
public holidays).
Secretary: J.C. Rutherford -
Tel: (01292) 477101.

Prestwick
St. Nicholas Golf Club
Grangemuir Road,
Prestwick KA9 1SN.
Tel: (01292) 477608.
Fax: (01292) 678570.

18 holes, length of course
5441m/5952 yds.
SSS 69
Charges: £30 round, £45 daily,
Sunday £35.
For advance reservations Tel:
(01292) 477608.
Caddy cars and catering
facilities are available.
Visitors are welcome Monday to
Friday & Sunday pm.
Secretary: G.B.S. Thomson -
Tel: (01292) 477608.
Golf Shop: (01292) 678559.

Skelmorie
Skelmorie Golf course
Belthglass Road,
Upper Skelmorie.
Tel: (01475) 520152.
13 holes, length of course
5056 m.
SSS 65
Charges: Mon - Fri (round) £13;
(daily) £17. Sat (round) £14;
(daily) £19.
Five days £60; Ten days £90.
Catering facilities are available
for visitors and parties.
Visitors are welcome all week,
except Saturdays.
Secretary: Mrs. A. Fahey -
Tel: (01475) 520774.

Stevenston
Ardeer Golf Club
Greenhead, Stevenston.
Tel: (01294) 464542.
18 holes, length of course
6409 yds.
SSS 71
Charges: On Application.
For advance reservations Tel:
(01294) 465316/464542
(secretary).
Caddy cars, practice area and
catering facilities are
available.
Visitors are welcome all week,
except Saturdays.
Secretary: P. Watson -
Tel: (01294) 465316..
Starter/Shop: R. Summerfield -
Tel: (01294) 601327.

Troon
*Darley Golf Course
Harling Drive,Troon KA10 6NF.

c/o South Ayrshire Council,
Burns House, Burns Statue
Square,
Ayr KA7 1UT.
Tel: (01292) 312464.
18 holes, length of course
6047 yds.
SSS 71
Charges: £13 round; £24
daily; 5-day tickets £80 .
For advance reservations
Tel: (01292) 312464.
A practice area, caddy cars
and catering facilities are
available.
Visitors are welcome all week.
Starters Office -
Tel: (01292) 312464.
Professional: Gordon McKinley-
Tel: (01292) 315566.

*Fullarton Golf Course
Harling Drive,
Troon KA10 6NF.
c/o South Ayrshire Council,
Burns House, Burns Statue
Square,
Ayr KA7 1UT.
Tel: (01292) 312464.
18 holes, length of course
4682 yds.
SSS 62
Charges: £11 round; £24
daily; 5-day ticket £80.
For advance reservations
Tel: (01292) 312464.
A practice area, caddy cars
and catering facilities are
available.
Visitors are welcome all week.
Starters Office -
Tel: (01292) 312464.
Professional: Gordon McKinlay-
Tel: (01292) 315566.

*Lochgreen Golf Course
Harling Drive,
Troon KA10 6NF.
c/o South Ayrshire Council,
Burns House, Burns Statue
Square,
Ayr KA7 1UT.
Tel: (01292) 312464.
18 holes, length of course
6478 yds.
SSS 71
Charges: £13 round, £24
daily, £80 weekly Mon-Fri.
For advance reservations

Tel: (01292) 312464.
A practice area, caddy cars
and catering facilities. Visitors
are welcome all week.
Starters Office-
Tel: (01292) 312464.
Professional: Gordon McKinley-
Tel: (01292) 315566.

Royal Troon Golf Club
Old Course (Championship)
Craigend Road, Troon KA10
6LD.
Tel: (01292) 311555.
18 holes, length of course
7097 yds.
SSS 73
Charges: £90 daily inc. lunch
(includes 1 round on both
courses). (No ladies or under-
18's).
Caddies, catering facilities -
please advise 1 week before-
hand- are available.
Visitors are welcome Mon,
Tues and Thurs only with
advance reservations & handi-
cap certificate.
Secretary: J.D. Montgomerie.
Professional: R. Brian
Anderson.

Royal Troon Golf Club
Portland Course
Crosbie Road,
Troon KA10 6EP.
Tel: (01292) 311555.
18 holes, length of course
6274 yds.
SSS 70
Charges: £60 daily inc. lunch
(composite fee).
Catering facilities are available.
Visitors are welcome Mon,
Tues and Thurs only with
advance reservations & handi-
cap certificate.
Secretary: J.D. Montgomerie.
Professional: R. Brian
Anderson.

Turnberry
Ailsa & Arran
Turnberry Hotel & Golf
Courses
Tel: (01655) 331000.
2 x 18 holes, length of courses
Ailsa 6976 yds. Par 70, Arran

6014 yds.
Par 68.
Practice area, caddies, trolleys on Arran course only. Dining faciliies are available.
Golf Operatons Manager: Mr. E.C. Bowman.
Professional: Mr. B. Gunson.

West Kilbride

West Kilbride Golf Club
Fullerton Drive,
West Kilbride KA23 9HT.
Tel: (01294) 823911.
18 holes, length of course
6247 yds.
SSS 71
Charges: On application.
For advance reservations Tel: (01294) 823042.
A practice area, caddy cars and catering facilities are available.
Visitors are welcome Monday to Friday.
Secretary: H.Armour - Tel: (01294) 823911.
Professional: G. Ross - Tel: (01294) 823042.

BANFFSHIRE
Banff

Duff House Royal Golf Club
The Barnyards,
Banff AB45 3SX.
Tel: (01261) 812062.
Fax: (01261) 812224.
18 holes, length of course
6161 yds.
SSS 70
Charges: On application.
For advance reservations Tel: (01261) 812062/812075.
A practice area, caddy cars and catering facilities are available.
Visitors are welcome all week (but within restricted times, as shown on Tee Booking sheets. Handicap Certificate preferred).
Secretary: J. Corbett - Tel: (01261) 812062.
Professional: R.S. Strachan - Tel: (01261) 812075.

Buckie

Buckpool Golf Club
Barhill Road, Buckie.
Tel/Fax: (01542) 832236.
18 holes, length of course
6257 yds.
SSS 70
Charges: Per round - £8 Mon-Fri; £10 Sat/Sun. Daily tickets - £12 Mon-Fri; £18 Sat/Sun. £40 weekly (Mon-Fri).
Juniors under 16 receive 50% reduction.
For advance reservations Tel: (01542) 832236.
Catering facilities are available.
Visitors are welcome daily.
Visiting parties are welcome by prior arrangement.
Club Administrator - Mrs. E. Cowie.

Strathlene Golf Club
Buckie AB56 2DJ.
Tel: (01542) 831798.
Charges: £10 round weekday, £15 weekday Day Ticket. £14 round weekend, £18 day weekend.
Essential to book for a tee-time at weekend. Golfing Societies welcome though by prior arrangement.
Secretary: G.M.C. Clark

Cullen

Cullen Golf Club
The Links, Cullen, Buckie AB56 2UU.
Tel: (01542) 840685.
18 holes, length of course 4610 yds.
SSS 62
Charges: Mon -Fri £7 round. Sat/Sun £9. Daily Tickets Mon-Fri £12, Sat/Sun £15. (All fees subject to review each November).
Juniors (2 sections) - under 16 and 16-18 years.
For advance reservations Tel: (01542) 840685.
A practice area, trolley carts, and practice putting green, catering facilities are available.
Visitors welcome all week (but

within restricted tee times as stated on Starter's Board for Club Competitions).
Visiting parties/golfing societies are welcome by prior arrangement. Handicap Certificate preferred but not essential.
Secretary: Ian Findlay-Tel: (01542) 840174.

Dufftown

Dufftown Golf Club
Methercluny, Tomintoul Road, Dufftown AB55 4BX..
Tel: (01340) 820325.
18 holes, length of course
5308 yds.
SSS 67
Charges: £10 round, £15 day all week.
Bar. Catering by arrangement.
Visitors are welcome all week.
Secretary: Mr. D.M. Smith - Tel: Evening (01340) 820033.
Day: (01340) 820227

Keith

Keith Golf Course
Fife Park,
Keith AB55 5DF.
Tel: (01542) 882469.
18 holes
SSS 68
Par 69.
Charges: Weekdays £12daily. Weekends £15 daily.
Visitors welcome, catering available. Parties by arrangement, advisable to telephone in advance weekends.
Hon. Secretary: D. Shepherd.

Macduff

Royal Tarlair Golf Club
Buchan Street, Macduff.
Tel: (01261) 832897.
18 holes, length of course
5866 yds.
SSS 68
Charges: £10 per round weekdays, £13 per round Sat/Sun. £15 per day weekdays, £20 per day Sat/Sun. Juniors

£6 per day. Adult weekly ticket £50, Junior weekly ticket £19.
For advance reservations Tel: (01261) 832897.
Caddy cars and catering facilities are available.
Visitors are welcome allweek.
Secretary: Mrs. Mary Law - Tel: (01261) 832897.

BERWICKSHIRE
Coldstream
Hirsel Golf Club
Kelso Road, Coldstream.
Tel: (01890) 882678.
18 holes, length of course 6092 yds.
SSS 72 Ladies
SSS 70 Men
Charges: £18 weekdays, £25 Sat/Sun
Caddy cars, practice area.
Full bar & restaurant facilities.
Visitors are welcome without reservation. Tee times may be booked with the starter Tel: (01890) 882678. Parties of 10 or over must book through the Secretary in advance.
Secretary: John C. Balfour, West Paddock, Duns Road, Coldstream.
Tel: (01890) 882233.

Duns

Duns Golf Club
Hardens Road, Duns.
Tel: (01361) 882194.
18 holes, length of course 6209 yds.
SSS 73 Ladies
SSS 70 Men
Charges: On application.
Catering facilities available (light snacks only).
Visitors welcome all week. Some restrictions, ring in advance.
Secretary: A. Campbell - Tel: (01361) 882717.

Eyemouth

Eyemouth Golf Club
Gunsgreen House, Eyemouth TD14 5DX.

Tel: (01890) 750551.
(Further details on application).

Lauder

Lauder Golf Club
Lauder.
Tel: (01578) 722526.
9 holes, length of course 6002 yds (18 holes).
SSS 70
Charges: On Application.
Practice area is available.
Visitors are welcome all week (some restrictions before noon on Sundays and 5pm Wednesdays).
Secretary: David Dickson - Tel: (01578) 722526.

CAITHNESS
Lybster
Lybster Golf Club
Main Street, Lybster, Caithness.
9 holes, length of course 1807 yds.
SSS 62
Charges: On Application.
Advance reservations are not necessary.
Visitors are welcome all week.
Secretary: Norman S. Fraser.

Reay

Reay Golf Club
Reay, Thurso KW14 7RE.
Tel: (01847) 811288.
18 holes, length of course 5372m/5876 yds.
SSS 69
Charges: £15 round/daily, £45 weekly.
A limited practice area is available.
Secretary: P. Peebles - Tel: (01847) 811537.

Thurso

Thurso Golf Club
Newlands of Geise, Thurso KW14 7LF..
Tel: (01847) 893807.
18 holes, length of course 5828 yds.

Par 69
Men SSS 69 Ladies 71
Heathland Course - most northerly 18 hole course on mainland - views of Pentland Firth and Orkney Island.
Bar open all day June, July, August - sandwiches available.
Visitors welcome. No booking. £15 per day. Juniors £8, £60 per week. Free golf at Pentland Hotel, Thurso, and John O'Groat Hotel, John O'Groats and Mackays Hotel, Wick. Country membership £60 p.a.

Wick

Wick Golf Club
Reiss, Caithness KW1 4RW.
Tel: (01955) 602726.
18 holes, length of course 5796 yds.
SSS 69
Charges: All week £15 daily; weekly £60; fortnightly £80. Juniors £3.
Visitors welcome without reservations.
Society meetings catered for.
Hon. Secretary: D.D. Shearer - Tel: (01955) 602935.

CLACKMANNAN-SHIRE

Alloa
Alloa Golf Club
Schaw Park, Sauchie, by Alloa.
Tel: (01259) 722745.
18 holes, length of course 6229 yds.
SSS 71.
Charges: On Application.
For advance bookings contact the Professional.
Practice areas, caddy cars and catering facilities are available.
Visitors and visiting parties are welcome.
Secretary: T. Crampton-Tel: (01259) 722745.
Professional: Bill Bennett - Tel: (01259) 724476.

Alva

Alva Golf Club
Beauclerc street, Alva.
Tel: (01259) 760431.
9 holes.
Charges: On application.
Limited opening for catering facilities.
Visitors are welcome all week.
Secretary: Mrs. A. McGuire - Tel: (01259) 760455.

Dollar

Dollar Golf Course
Brewlands House,
Dollar FK14 7EA.
Tel: (01259) 742400.
18 holes, length of course 5144 yds.
SSS 66
Charges (Mon-Fri) £10 round.
Weekday Day Ticket £14. £18.50 (Sat/Sun).
For advance reservations Tel: (01259) 742400.
Catering facilities are available, except Tuesdays.
Visitors are welcome all week.
Secretary: Mr. J.C. Brown - Tel: (01259) 742400.

Kincardine on Forth
Tulliallan Golf Club
Alloa Road,
Kincardine, by Alloa.
Tel: (01259) 730396.
18 holes, length of course 5459m/5965 yds.
SSS 69
Charges: £15 round (Mon-Fri), £20 (Sat/Sun).
£25 daily (Mon-Fri), £30 (Sat/Sun).
For advance reservations: Tel: (01259) 730798.
Caddy cars and catering facilities are available.
Visitors are welcome by prior arrangement.
Secretary: J.S. McDowall - Tel: (01324) 485420.
Professional: Steve Kelly - Tel: (01259) 730798.

Muckhart

Muckhart Golf Club
by Dollar.
Tel: (01259) 781423.
18 holes, length of course 6034 yds.
SSS 70
Charges: £15 round (Mon-Fri), £22 (Sat/Sun). £22 Daily (Mon-Fri), £30 (Sat/Sun).
Caddy cars and catering facilities are available.
Secretary: A.B. Robertson.
Professional: Mr. K. Salmoni.

Tillicoultry

Tillicoultry Golf Course
Alva Road, Tillicoultry.
9 holes, length of course 4518m/5266 yds (18 holes).
SSS 66
Charges: £10 round Mon-Fri (18 holes), £12 after 4pm. Sat-Sun £15 round.
For advance reservations Tel: (01259) 750124.
A practice area and catering facilities are available.
Visitors are welcome all week (except competition days).
Secretary: Mr. R. Whitehead - Tel: (01259) 750124.

DUMFRIESSHIRE
Annan
Powfoot Golf Club
Powfoot, Annan DG12 5QE.
Tel/Fax: (01461) 700276.
18 holes, length of course 6010 yds.
SSS 70
Charges: £20 per round, £27 per day.
For advance reservations Tel: (01461) 700276.
A practice area, caddy cars and catering facilities are available.
Visitors are welcome all week except Sat and before 2pm on Sun.
Manager: B.W. Sutherland MBE Tel: (01461) 700276.
Professional: Gareth Dick - Tel: (01461) 700327.

Dumfries

Crichton Golf Club,
Bankend Road,
Dumfries DG1 4TH.
Tel/Fax: (01387) 247894.
9 holes, length of course 2,976 yds.
SSS 69 White
SSS 68 Blue
Charges: On Application.
For advance reservations Tel: (01387) 247894.
Catering facilities are available.
Visitors are welcome: Mon, Wed, Fri, Sat & Sun.

Dumfries and County Golf Club
Edinburgh Road,
Dumfries DG1 1JX.
Tel: (01387) 253585.
18 holes, length of course 5928 yds.
SSS 68
Charges: On Application.
A practice area, caddy carts and catering facilities are available.
Visitors are welcome all week, except Saturdays.
Secretary: E.C. Pringle - Tel: (01387) 253585.
Professional: Shop -Tel: (01387) 268918.

Dumfries and Galloway Golf Club
2 Laurieston Avenue,
Dumfries DG2 7NY.
Tel: (01387) 253582.
18 holes, length of course 5803 yds
SSS 68
Charges: £21 round, £21 daily, £60 weekly.
For advance reservations Tel: (01387) 253582.
Practice area, caddy cars and catering facilities available.
Visitors welcome weekdays except Tuesday.
Secretary: Jack Donnachie - Tel: (01387) 263848.
Professional: Joe Ferguson - Tel: (01387) 256902.

Langholm

Langholm Golf Course
Whitaside, Langholm
DG13 OMN.
Tel: (01387) 381247.
9 holes, length of course
5744 yds.
SSS 68
Charges: £10 round/daily, £50
weekly.
Practice area is available.
Visitors are welcome all week.
Secretary: W.J. Wilson -
Tel: (01387) 380673.

Lochmaben

Lochmaben Golf Club
Castlehillgate,
Lochmaben,
Lockerbie DG11 1NT.
Tel: (01387) 810552.
18 holes, length of course
4863m/5336 yds.
SSS 67
Charges: On Application.
A practice area and catering is
available.
Visitors are welcome -
weekdays before 5pm and
weekends by arrangement.
Hon. Secretary: J.M. Dickie -
Tel: (01387) 810713.

Lockerbie

Hoddom Castle Golf Club
Hoddom Castle, Hoddom,
Lockerbie.
Tel: (01576) 300251.
9 holes, length of course 2320m
SSS 33
Charges: On Application.
For advance reservations
Tel: (01576) 300251.
Catering facilities available
and visitors welcome all week.

Lockerbie Golf Club
Corrie Road, Lockerbie.
Tel: (01576) 203363.
18 holes, length of course
5614 yds.
SSS 67
Charges: £168Mon-Fri; £22 Sat
daily; £18 per round Sun.
A practice area and catering
facilities are available.
Visitors are welcome all week.
Secretary: J. Thomson -
Tel/Fax: (01576) 203363.

Moffat

The Moffat Golf Club
Coatshill, Moffat DG10 9SB.
Tel: (01683) 220020.
18 holes, length of course
5218 yds.
SSS 66
Charges: On application.
For advance reservations Tel:
(01683) 220020.
Caddy cars and catering
facilities are available.
Visitors are welcome, except
Wednesday after 12 noon.
Secretary: T.A. Rankin -
Tel: (01683) 220020.

Sanquhar

Euchan Golf Course
Sanquhar.
Tel: (01659) 50577.
9 holes, length of course
5144m (18 holes).
SSS 68
Charges: On Application.
For advance reservations Tel:
(01659) 58181.
Catering facilities (advance
notice by parties) are
available.
Visitors are welcome all week.
Secretary: Mrs. J. Murray -
Tel: (01659) 58181.

Southerness

Southerness Golf Club
Southerness,
Dumfries DG2 8AZ.
Tel: (01387) 880677.
18 holes, length of course
6564 yds.
SSS 73
Charges: £25 (Mon-Fri) daily,
£35 (weekend). £100 weekly
(Mon-Fri).
For advance reservations Tel:
(01387) 880677. Fax: (01387)
880644.
A practice area, caddy cars
and catering facilities are
available.
Visitors - members of
recognised golf clubs only are
welcome all week.
Secretary: W.D. Ramage -
Tel: (01387) 880677.
Fax: (01387) 880644.
5444m/5957 yds.

Thornhill

Thornhill Golf Club
Thornhill.
Tel: (01848) 330546.
18 holes, length of course
6085 yds.
SSS 70
Par 71
Charges: £20weekdays,
£24 weekends.
For advance reservations Tel:
(01848) 330546 (Club
Steward).
A practice area and catering
facilities are available.
Visitors are welcome all week.
Secretary: J.F.K. Crichton.

DUMBARTONSHIRE

Alexandria

Vale of Leven Golf Club
Northfield Road, Bonhill.
Tel: (01389) 752351.
18 holes, length of course
5165 yds
SSS 66
Charges: Mon-Fri £12 round,
£18 day ticket. Weekends:
£16 round, £24 day ticket (1996
prices).
Catering facilities are avail-
able.
Visitors are welcome all week.
No discount for parties.
Secretary: J. Stewart -
18 Gallacher Crescent,
Balloch G83 8HN.
Tel: (01389) 757691.

Bearsden

Bearsden Golf Club
Thorn Road,
Bearsden, Glasgow.
Tel: 0141-942 2351.
9 holes, length of course
6014 yds.
SSS 69
Charges: On application.
Visitors are welcome, but must
be introduced by a member.
Secretary: Mr. J.R. Mercer -
Tel: 0141-942 2351.

Douglas Park Golf Club
Hillfoot, Bearsden.
Tel: 0141-942 2220.
18 holes, length of course

SSS 69
Charges: £21 round, £28 daily.
For advance reservations Tel:
0141-942 2220.
Caddy cars and catering
facilities are available.
Visiting parties by prior
arrangement are welcome
Wednesdays and Thursdays.
Secretary: D.N. Nicolson -
Tel: 0141-942 2220.
Professional: D. Scott -
Tel: 0141-942 1482.

Glasgow Golf Club
Killermont,
Bearsden,
Glasgow.
Tel: 0141-942 2011.
Fax: 0141-942 0770.
18 holes, length of course
5456m/5968 yds.
SSS 69
Charges: On application.
Visitors by member's
introduction.
Professional: Jack Steven -
Tel: 0141-942 8507.

Windyhill Golf Club
Baljaffray Road,
Bearsden G61 4QQ.
Tel: 0141-942 2349.
18 holes, length of course
6254 yds.
SSS 70
Charges: £20 round, £20 daily,
£80 weekly.
For advance reservations
Tel: 0141-942 5874.
A practice area, caddies, caddy
cars and catering facilities are
available.
Visitors are welcome Mon-Fri.
Secretary: Brian Davidson -
Tel: 0141-942 2349.
Fax: 0141-942 5874.
Professional: Gary Collinson -
Tel: 0141-942 7157.

Clydebank

**Clydebank & District Golf
Club**
Glasgow Road, Hardgate,
Clydebank G81 5QY.
Tel: (01389) 873289.
18 holes, length of course
5326m/5825 yds.
SSS 68
Charges: £15 round.
For advance reservations Tel:

Professional (01389) 878686.
A practice area and catering
facilities are available.
Visitors are welcome Mon-Fri
Secretary: W. Manson -
Tel: (01389) 872832.
Professional: David Pirie -
Tel: (01389) 878686.

Cumbernauld

*Palacerigg Golf Club
Palacerigg Country Park,
Cumbernauld G67.
Tel: (01236) 734969.
18 holes, length of course
5894m/6444 yds.
SSS 71
Charges: On Application.
For advance reservations Tel:
(01236) 721461.
A practice area and catering
facilities are available.
Visitors are welcome all week.
Secretary: David S.A. Cooper -
Tel: (01236) 734969.

**Westerwood Hotel, Golf &
Country Club**
Westerwood,
1 St. Andrews Drive,
Cumbernauld G68
OEW.
Tel: (01236) 457171.
18 holes, length of course
6139m/6721 yds.
SSS 73
Par 72
Charges: On application.
For advance reservations Tel:
(01236) 452772.
Caddy cars, practice area and
catering facilities are
available.
Visitors are welcome all week.

Dullatur

Dullatur Golf Club
Glen Douglas Drive,
Craigmarloch, Cumbernauld.
Tel: (01236) 723230.

Carrickstone Course
 18 hole courses, length of
course 6204 yds.
SSS 70

Antonine Course
18 holes, length of course 5940
yds.

SSS 69
Charges: On Application.
For advance reservations Tel:
(01236) 723230.
Caddy cars, practice area and
catering facilities are
available.
Visitors are welcome Mon-Fri
(except 1st Wed in month &
public holidays).
Secretary: Mrs C. Millar -
Tel: (01236) 723230.
Professional: D. Sinclair -
Tel: (01236) 723230.

Dumbarton

Cardross Golf Club
Main Road, Cardross,
Dumbarton G82 5LB.
Tel: (01389) 841213.
18 holes, length of course
6469 yds.
SSS 72
Charges: £22 round,
£32 day ticket.
For advance reservations Tel:
(01389) 841350.
Caddy cars, practice area and
catering facilities are
available.
Visitors welcome weekdays
only.
Secretary: I.T. Waugh -
Tel: (01389) 841754.

Dumbarton Golf Course
Overtorn Avenue,
Broadmeadow, Dumbarton.
Tel: (01389) 732830.
(Further details on
application).

Helensburgh

Helensburgh Golf Club
25 East Abercromby Street,
Helensburgh
Tel: (01436) 674173.
(Further details on
application).

Kirkintilloch

Hayston Golf Club
Campsie Road,
Kirkintilloch G66 1RN.
Tel: 0141-776 1244.
18 holes, length of course
5808m/6042 yds.
SSS 70

Charges: On Application.
For advance reservations Tel:
0141-775 0723.
A practice area, caddy cars
and catering facilities are
available.
Secretary: J.V. Carmichael -
Tel: 0141-775 0723.
Professional: Mr. S. Barnett -
Tel: 0141-775 0882.

Kirkintilloch Golf Club
Todhill, Campsie Road,
Kirkintilloch G66 1RN.
Tel: 0141-776 1256.
(Further details on
application).

Milngavie

Clober Golf Club
Craigton Road,
Milngavie.
Tel: 0141-956 6963.
18 holes, length of course
5068 yds.
SSS 65
Charges: £12 per round.
Caddy cars and catering
facilities are available.
Visitors welcome until 4.30pm
Mon to Thurs, 4pm on Fri
(last Tues monthly 4pm).
Interim Secretary: T.S. Arthur
-
Tel: 0141-955 0382.

Dougalston Golf Course
Strathblane Road,
Milngavie, Glasgow.
Tel: 0141-956 5750.
(Further details on
application).
Office Secretary: Maureen
Young - Tel: 0141-956 5750.

Hilton Park Golf Club
Stockmuir Road,
Milngavie G62 7HB.
Tel: 0141-956 4657.
2 x 18 hole courses, length of
courses 6054 and 5374 yds.
SSS 70 and 66
Charges: On application.
Caddy cars, practice area and
catering facilities are
available.
Visitors are welcome by prior
arrangement.
Monday-Friday, except 2nd
and 4th Tuesdays of each
month.

Secretary: Mrs. J.A. Warnock -
Tel: 0141-956 4657.
Professional:
Mr. Wm. McCondichie -
Tel: 0141-956 5125.

Milngavie Golf Club
Laighpark, Milngavie,
Glasgow G62 8EP.
Tel: 0141-956 1619.
18 holes, length of course
5818 yds.
SSS 68
Charges: On Application.
A practice area and catering
facilities are available.
Visitors are welcome if intro-
duced by a member.
Secretary: Ms S. McInnes -
Tel: 0141-956 1619.

FIFE
Aberdour

Aberdour Golf Club
Seaside Place,
Aberdour KY3 OTX.
Tel: (01383) 860688.
18 holes, length of course
5460 yds.
SSS 66
Charges: £17 round (£12 win-
ter), £28 day. Weekend no
round tickets.
For advance reservations
Tel: (01383) 860256
Catering facilities are
available.
Visitors are welcome all week.
Secretary: J.J. Train -
Tel: (01383) 860080.
Professional: G. MacCallum -
Tel: (01383) 860256.

Anstruther

Anstruther Golf Club
Marsfield, Shore Road,
Anstruther.
Tel: (01333) 310956.
9 holes, length of course
4504m.
SSS 63
Charges: £12 weekdays, £15
weekend.
For advance reservations Tel:
(01333) 310956.
Catering facilities are avail-
able.
Visitors are welcome.
Secretary: J.F. MacLeod.

Burntisland

Burntisland Golf House Club
Dodhead, Burntisland.
Tel: (01592) 874093.
18 holes, length of course
5391m/5897 yds.
SSS 69
Charges: £15 (weekday)
round, £25 (Sat/Sun) round.
£23 (weekday) daily, £35 (Sat/
Sun) daily. Weekly by
arrangement.
For advance reservations Tel:
(01592) 873247/874093.
A practice area, caddy cars
and catering facilities are
available.
Visitors are welcome all week.
Manager: W. Taylor -
Tel: (01592) 874093.
Professional:
Mr. Jacky Montgomery -
Tel: (01592) 873247.

Cardenden

*Auchterderran Golf Club
Woodend Road,
Cardenden KY5 ONH.
Tel: (01592) 721579 Clubhouse.
9 holes, length of course
5250 yds.
SSS 66
Charges £9 daily, weekdays.
£12.50 daily, weekends.
Meals available by advance
booking.
Bar snacks Mon, Wed, Fri, Sat
& Sun.
Bar facilities Mon, Wed, Fri,
Sat & Sun.
Visitors welcome. Visiting par-
ties exc. Sat.

Cowdenbeath

Dora Golf Course
Seco Place, Cowdenbeath.
Tel: (01383) 511918.
2 x 9 holes, length of each
course 2981m/3261 yds.
SSS 70
Charges: Weekdays £7.50 day,
£10.50 day weekend.
For advance reservations: -
Tel: (01383) 511918
(Clubhouse).
Practice area, caddy cars and
catering facilities available.

Visitors welcome all week.
Secretary: Duncan Ferguson -
Tel: (01383) 511918
(Clubhouse).

Crail

Crail Golfing Society
Balcomie Club House,
Fifeness, Crail
KY10 3XN.
Tel: (01333) 450686.
18 holes, length of course
5922 yds.
SSS 69
Charges: £19 round, £30 daily,
weekday. £24 round, £38
daily, weekend (1996).
Caddies, caddy cars, practice
area and catering facilities are
possible.
Visitors are welcome.
Advance bookings for parties
are available.
Manager: Jim Horsfield -
Tel: (01333) 450686.
Fax: (01333) 450416.
Professional: G. Lennie -
Tel: (01333) 450278 &
(01333) 450960.

Cupar

Cupar Golf Club
Hilltarvit, Cupar.
Tel: (01334) 653549.
2 x 9 holes, length of course
5074 yds.
SSS 65
Par 68
Charges: Adult £12 day, £15
Sunday. Juvenile £5 day.
Family Day Ticket £25.Weekly
Ticket £50.
Catering facilities are
available.
Visitors welcome except
Saturdays.
Secretary: J.M. Houston -
Tel: (01334) 654101.

Dunfermline

Canmore Golf Club
Venturefair, Dunfermline.
Tel: (01383) 724969.
(Further details from the
Secretary on (01383)
726098).

Dunfermline Golf Club
Pitfirrane Crossford,
Dunfermline KY12 8QW.
18 holes, length of course
6126 yds.
SSS 70
Charges: £20 round, £28 daily
Mon-Fri.£25 round, £35 daily
Sun.
For advance reservations Tel:
Professional: S. Craig - (01383)
729061 (casual visitor);
Societies phone Secretary.
Clubhouse category 'A' Listed
building.
Caddy cars, practice area and
catering facilities are
available.
Visitors are welcome
Mon. to Fri.
Secretary: R. De Rose -
Tel: (01383) 723534.

Pitreavie (Dunfermline)
Golf
Club
Queensferry Road,
Dunfermline KY11 5PR.
Tel: (01383) 722591.
18 holes, length of course
5565m/6086 yds.
SSS 69
Charges: Weekdays £18
round, £24 daily. Weekends
£35 daily - no round tickets.
For advance reservations -
Casual visitors Tel: (01383)
723151, Parties, Societies etc.
Tel: (01383) 722591.
A practice area, caddy cars
and catering facilities are
available.
Visitors are welcome all week.
Secretary: Mr. R.T. Mitchell -
Tel: (01383) 722591.
Professional: Colin Mitchell -
Tel: (01383) 723151.

Elie

Earlsferry Thistle Golf Club
Melon Park, Elie.
(further details on
application).

'The Golf House Club'
Elie, Fife KY9 1AS.
Tel: (01333) 330301.
18 holes, length of course
6241 yds.
SSS 70
Charges: On Application.

For advance reservations Tel:
(01333) 330301.
Catering facilities are
available.
Visitors are welcome
midweek.
Secretary: A. Sneddon -
Tel: (01333) 330301.
Professional: Robin Wilson -
Tel: (01333) 330955.

Falkland

*Falkland Golf Course
The Myre, Falkland.
Tel: (01337) 857404.
9 holes, length of course
2384m/2608 yds.
SSS 66 (18)
Charges: On Application.
Visitors are welcome. Parties
are welcome by prior
arrangement.
Secretary: Mrs. H.H.
Horsburgh - Tel: (01592)
756075.

Glenrothes

Balbirnie Park Golf Club
Balbirnie Park, Markinch,
by Glenrothes KY7 6NR.
Tel: (01592) 612095.
18 holes, length of course
6210 yds.
SSS 70
Charges: On application.
For advance reservations
contact: A.D. Gordon,
Assistant Secretary
Tel: (01592) 752006.
Full catering facilities - con-
tact:
Club Steward/Stewardess:
John & Heather Gough.
Tel: (01592) 612095.
Visitors welcome.
Tee bookings required.
Hon.Secretary:P. Todhunter -
Tel: (01592) 752006.

*Glenrothes Golf Club
Golf Course Road,
Glenrothes KY6 2LA.
Tel: (01592) 758686.
Length of course
5984m/6444 yds.
SSS 71
Charges: £12 round, £20
daily (weekdays). £16 round,
£25 daily (weekends).

For advance reservations
Tel: (01592) 754561,
min. 12 players.
A practice area and catering
facilities are available.
Visitors are welcome all week.
Hon. Secretary: Mrs. P.V.
Landells - Tel: (01592) 754561.

Kinghorn

*Kinghorn Municipal Golf Club
c/o Fife Council Ground
Maintenance Services,
Kinghorn.
Tel: (01592) 412690.
18 holes, length of course
4544m/4969 yds.
SSS 67
Par 65
Charges: On application.
Catering facilities through
Clubmistress Tel: (01592)
890345.
Secretary: J.P. Robertson -
Tel: (01592) 203397.

Kirkcaldy

*Dunnikier Park Golf Course
Dunnikier Way,
Kirkcaldy.
Tel: (01592) 261599.
18 holes, length of course
6036m/6601 yds.
SSS 72
Charges: £13 round, £22 daily
(Mon-Fri). £18 round, £27
daily (Sat/Sun).
A practice area, caddy cars
and catering facilities are
available.
Professional: G. Whyte -
Tel: (01592) 642121.
Secretary: Mr. R.A. Waddell -
Tel: (01592) 200627.

Kirkcaldy Golf Club
Balwearie Road,
Kirkcaldy KY2 5LT.
Tel: (01592) 260370.
18 holes, length of course
6004 yds.
SSS 69
Charges: £15 round
(weekdays), £20 (weekends).
£20 daily (weekdays), £30
weekends.
For advance reservations Tel:

(01592) 205240/203258.
A practice area, caddy cars
and bar and full catering facili-
ties are
available.
Visitors are welcome all week,
except Saturdays and limited
Tuesdays.
Secretary: Alistair Thomson -
Tel: (01592) 205240.
Professional: Mr. Scott McKay -
Tel: (01592) 203258.

Ladybank

Ladybank Golf Club
Annsmuir, Ladybank.
Tel: (01337) 830814/830725.
18 holes, length of course
6641 yds.
SSS 72
Charges: Nov/April - £19 per
round, £27 daily. April/Sept. -
£28
per round,
£38 daily. Weekly £120.
For advance reservations Tel:
(01337) 830814.
Caddy cars, a practice area
and catering facilities are
available.
Visitors are welcome all week,
except Saturdays.
Secretary: I.F. Sproule -
Tel: (01337) 830814.
Professional: M. Gray -
Tel: (01337) 830725.
E-mail: ladybankgc@aol.com

Leslie

Leslie Golf Club
Balsillie Laws,
Leslie, Glenrothes.
Tel: (01592) 620040.
9 holes, length of course
4516m/4940 yds.
SSS 64
Charges: On Application.
Bar facilities from
7.30pm-11.00pm.
Visitors are welcome all week.
Secretary: G. Lewis -

Leuchars

Drumoig Golf Club & Hotel
Drumoig, Leuchars,
St. Andrews KY16 OBE.
Tel: (01382) 541800.
18 holes, length of course

6420m/7017 yds.
SSS 72
Charges: £20-£25 round.
For advance reservations:
(01382) 541800.
Caddy Trollies, practice area,
restaurant and bar facilities
available.
Visitors welcome all week.
Secretary: Tel: (01382) 541800.
Professional: (01382) 541800.

St. Michael's Golf Club
Leuchars.
Tel: (01334) 839365/838666.
18 holes, length of course
(Blue tees) 5563 yds.
SSS 67 (Par 70).
Charges: £15 per round
under 16's £7.50.
For Society reservations con-
tact
Golf Club.
Caddy trolleys, bar and cater-
ing
facilities are available.
Visitors are welcome all week
but not before 1pm on
Sundays.
Secretary: R. Smith.

Leven

Leven Links Golf Course
The Promenade,
Leven KY8 4HS.
Tel: (01333) 428859.
18 holes, length of course
6436 yds.
SSS 70
Charges: On application.
For advance reservations Tel:
(01333) 428859/421390.
Caddy cars and catering facili-
ties are available.
Visitors are welcome
Sunday to Friday.
Secretary: A. Herd Esq. -
Tel: (01333) 428859.

*Scoonie Golf Club
North Links,
Leven KY8 4SP.
Tel: (01333) 307007.
Fax: (01333) 307008.
18 holes, length of course
4967m.
SSS 65
Charges: On Application.
Caddy cars and full catering
facilities are available.

Visitors welcome. Visiting parties not accepted on Saturdays.
Secretary: Mr. S. Kuczerepa -
Tel: (01333) 427057.

Lochgelly

Lochgelly Golf Course
Lochgelly Golf Club
Cartmore Road, Lochgelly KY5
9PB.
Tel: (01592) 780174.
(Further details on
application).

Lundin Links
Lundin Golf Club
Golf Road,
Lundin Links, Leven KY8 6BA.
Tel: (01333) 320202.
18 holes, length of course
6394 yds.
SSS 71
Charges: £27 per round, £36
per day. Other charges on
application.
For advance reservations Tel:
(01333) 320202.
Golf trolleys, practice area and
catering facilities are
available.
Visitors: Weekdays between
9am-3.30pm (3pm Fri). After
2.30 Sat (£36 per round). No
visitors Sun.
Secretary: D.R. Thomson -
Tel: (01333) 320202.
Fax: (01333) 329743.
Professional: D.K. Webster -
Tel: (01333) 320051.

Lundin Ladies Golf Club
Woodlielea Road,
Lundin Links,
Leven KY8 6AR.
9 holes, length of course
2365 yds.
SSS 67
Charges: £8 weekdays,
£9.50 weekends daily.
For advance reservations Tel:
(01333) 320832 (Clubhouse) or
write to secretary.
A few caddy cars are
available.
Visitors are welcome all week
except Wednesdays April-
August
(competitions).
Secretary:
Mrs. Elizabeth Davidson.

St. Andrews

St. Andrews Links
Management Committee.
Tel: (01334) 466666.
(Further details on
application).

***St. Andrews Balgove
Course**
9 holes beginners' course.
18 holes.
Charges: £7 (18 holes High
Season),
£5 (18 holes Low Season)
round.
Visitors are welcome, except
Saturdays.
For advance reservations Tel:
(01334) 466666.

*St. Andrews Eden Course
18 holes, length of course
5588m/6112 yds.
SSS 70
Charges: £20 round (High
Season - 1 Apr - 31 Oct).
£16 round (Low Season - 1 Nov
-1 Mar).
3 day pass £75. Weekly £150.
Children's rate: 3-day pass:
£37, weekly pass: £75. These
tickets are valid on all courses
except the Old.
For advance reservations Tel:
(01334) 466666.
Caddies and trolleys are available.

***St. Andrews Jubilee
Course**
18 holes, length of course
6223m/6805 yds.
SSS 73
Charges: £25 High Season
(1 Apr-31 Oct). £20 Low
Season (1 Nov - 31 Mar).
Weekly £150. 3 day pass £75 .
Children's rates: 3 day pass:
£37, weekly pass £75. These
tickets are valid on all courses
except the Old.
For advance reservations Tel:
(01334) 466666.
Caddies and trolleys available.

*St. Andrews New Course
18 holes, length of course
6038m/6604 yds.
SSS 72
Charges: £30 High Season
(Apr 1-Oct 31), £24 Low

Season (Nov 1-Mar 31).
3 day pass: £75, week pass:
£150. Children's Rate: 3 Day
Pass: £37, weekly pass: £75.
These tickets are vailid on all
courses except the Old.
For advance reservations Tel:
(01334) 466666.
Caddies and trolleys available.
Links Manager: Ian Forbes -
Tel: (01334) 466666.

*St. Andrews Old Course
18 holes, length of course
6004m/6566 yds.
SSS 72
Charges: £70 High Season
(April 1- Oct. 31). £50 in
Nov/£35 Dec - March (mats in
use).
season (1 Nov - March 31).
(Closed Sunday).
For advance reservations Tel:
(01334) 466666.
Caddies are available.
A handicap certificate or
letter of introduction is
required from visitors.
Links Manager: Ian Forbes -
Tel: (01334) 466666.

*Strathtyrum Course
18 holes, length of course
4661m/5094 yds.
SSS 64
Charges: £15 per round High
Season,
£13 per round low season.
3 Day Pass £75 , weekly pass:
£150 low season.
Caddies and trolleys available.
Visitors are welcome, except
Saturdays.
Links Manager: Ian Forbes -
Tel: (01334) 466666.

The New Golf Club
3/5 Gibson Place,
St. Andrews.
Tel: (01334) 473426.
Changing facilities with lockers
and showers units. Lounge bar
and Restaurant.
Secretary: A.J. Dochard -
Tel: (01334) 473426
    (01334) 472262.
Fax: (01334) 477570.

Saline

Saline Golf Club
Kinneddar Hill,
Saline.
Tel: (01383) 852591.
9 holes, length of course
5302 yds.
SSS 66
Charges: £9 per day Mon-Fri.
£11 per day Sun.
For advance reservations Tel:
Clubhouse (01383) 852591.
Practice area, catering
facilities are available.
Visitors are welcome all week,
except Saturdays.
Secretary: R. Hutchison -
Tel: (01383) 852344.

Tayport

Scotscraig Golf Club
Golf Road, Tayport DD6
9DZ.
Tel: (01382) 552515.
18 holes, length of course
6550 yds.
SSS 72
Charges: On application.
Caddies by arrangement,
caddy cars, practice area and
catering facilities are
available.
Visitors are welcome on
weekdays, or on weekends by
prior arrangement.
Secretary: K. Gourlay.

Thornton
Thornton Golf Club

Station Road,
Thornton KY1 4DW.
Tel: (01592) 771111.
Fax: (01592) 774955.
18 holes, length of course
5560m/6177 yds.
SSS 69
Charges: £14 weekdays, £20
weekends round; £20
weekdays, £30 weekends
daily. Juniors 50% off adult
rate.
For advance reservations Tel:
(01592) 771111.
New clubhouse built for 1997
season.
Practice area and catering
facilities are available.
Visitors are welcome all week.

Secretary: B.S.L. Main -
Tel: (01592) 771111.

INVERNESS-SHIRE
Aigas

Aigas Golf Course,
Aigas, by Beauly,
Inverness-shire.
Tel: (01463) 782942.
9 holes, length of course
2439 yds.
SSS 64
Charges: £7 (9 holes) week-
days,
£11 daily weekends, weekdays,
£42 weekly.
Caddy cars and catering facili-
ties
are available.
For advance reservations Tel:
(01463) 782942/782423.
Secretary: P. Masheter -
Tel: (01463) 782423.

Arisaig

Traigh Golf Course
Traigh, Arisaig.
Tel: (01687) 450337.
9 holes, length of course
2405 yds.
SSS 65
Charges: £10 daily, £40 weekly.
Clubs for hire.
Visitors are welcome all week.
Manager: Bill Henderson -
Tel: (01687) 450645.

Boat of Garten

Boat of Garten Golf Club
Boat of Garten PH24 3BQ.
Tel: (01479) 831282.
Fax: (01479) 831523.
18 holes, length of course
5866 yds.
SSS 69
Charges: Mon-Fri £20 daily,
Sat/Sun £25 daily. £90 weekly.
1997 charges.
For advance reservations Tel:
(01479) 831282
(starting sheet used every day).
Caddies, caddy cars and
catering facilities are
available.
Visitors are welcome.
Secretary: Paddy Smyth.

Carrbridge

Carrbridge Golf Club
Carrbridge.
Tel: (01479) 841623.
9 holes, length of course
5400 yds.
SSS 68
Charges: £10 Mon-Fri (except
July, Aug, Sept). £11 Mon-Fri
(July, Aug, Sept), £12 Sat/Sun
(1997). (Charges same as
1996).
For advance reservations Tel:
Clubhouse (01479) 841623.
Caddy cars and light catering
facilities available.
Visitors welcome all week
except Wed. after 5pm.
Restrictions most Suns.
Secretary: Mrs. A.T. Baird -
Tel: (01479) 841506.

Fort Augustus

Fort Augustus Golf Club
Markethill, Fort Augustus.
9 holes (18 tees), length of
course 5454 yds.
SSS 67
Charges: £10 daily.
For advance reservations Tel:
(01320) 366309/366660.
Clubs for hire. Caddy cars
available.
Visitors are welcome all week,
except Saturday afternoons.
Lounge bar.
Secretary: H. Fraser -
Tel: (01320) 366309.

Fort William

Fort William Golf Club
North Road, Torlundy,
Fort William.
Tel: (01397) 704464.
18 holes, length of course
6217 yds.
SSS 71
Charges: £12 daily.
Visitors are welcome all week.
Secretary: Mr. G. Bales.

Inverness

Castle Heather Golf Club
Castle Heather,
Inverness IV1 2AA.
Tel: (01463) 713335.
18 holes, length of course

6772m
SSS 72
Charges: £20/£25 Daily.
For advance reservations Tel:
(01463) 713334.
A practice area, caddies, caddy
cars and catering facilities are
available.
Visitors welcome all week.
Secretary: Gary Thompson -
Tel: (01463) 713335.
Professional: Martin Piggott -
Tel: (01463) 713334.

Inverness Golf Club
Culcabock Road,
Inverness IV2 3XQ.
Tel: (01463) 239882.
18 holes, length of course
5694m/6226 yds.
SSS 70
Charges: £25 round, £34 day
ticket (weekdays). £30 round,
£40 day ticket (Sat/Sun &
public hols.) £90 weekly
ticket.
For advance reservations Tel:
(01463) 239882 or 231989.
A practice area, caddy cars,
caddies and catering facilities
are available.
Visitors are welcome all week
(restrictions on Saturdays).
Secretary: G.B. Thomson -
Tel: (01463) 231989.
Professional: A.P. Thomson.

*Torvean Golf Club
Glenurquhart Road,
Inverness.
Tel: (01463) 225651.
18 holes, length of course
5784 yds.
SSS 68
Par 69
Charges: £10.10 (weekdays),
£11.60 (weekends) per round.
£13.40 (weekdays), £15.10
(weekends) daily.
For advance reservations Tel:
(01463) 711434.
Visitors are welcome all week
- but booking is advisable.
Secretary: Mrs. K.M. Gray -
Tel: (01463) 225651.

Kingussie

Kingussie Golf Club
Gynack Road, Kingussie.
Tel: Clubhouse (01540)
661374.

Sec. Office (01540)
661600.
18 holes, length of course
5079m/5555 yds.
SSS 68
Charges: On Application.
For advance reservations Tel:
(01540) 661600/661374.
Caddy cars and catering
facilities are available.
Visitors are welcome all week.
Secretary: N.D. MacWilliam -
Tel: (01540) 661600.

Nethy Bridge

Abernethy Golf Club
Nethy Bridge PH25 3EB.
Tel: (01479) 821305.
(Further details on
application).

Newtonmore

Newtonmore Golf Club
Newtonmore PH20 1AT.
Tel: Clubhouse (01540) 673328
Tel/Fax: (01540) 673878.
18 holes length of course 6029
yds.
SSS 69
Caddy cars & buggies avail-
able.
Catering every day except
Tuesdays. Visitors most wel-
come.
Charges: On Application.
For advance reservations &
group bookings contact:
Secretary: R.J. Cheyne -
Tel: (01540) 673878.
Professional: R. Henderson -
Tel: (01540) 673611.

Spean Bridge

Spean Bridge Golf Club
Spean Bridge.
Tel: (01397) 703379.
9 holes, length of course
2203 yds.
SSS 62
Charges: On Application.
Visitors are welcome all week
(except Tuesdays after 5pm).
Secretary: John Lennan -
Tel: (01397) 703379.

KINCARDINESHIRE
Auchenblae

*Auchenblae Golf Club
Auchenblae,
Laurencekirk AB30 1AA.
Tel: (01561) 320002.
9 holes, length of course
2174 yds.
SSS 30
Charges: On Application.
OAP's and juniors half price.
Visitors are welcome all week
apart from Weds & Fri
evenings (5.30pm-9pm).
Secretary:J. McNicoll -
Tel: (01561) 330678.

Banchory
Banchory Golf Club
Kinneskie Road, Banchory.
Tel: (01330) 822365.
18 holes, length of course
5775 yds.
Charges: On Application.
For advance reservations Tel:
(01330) 822447.
A practice area, caddy cars and
catering facilities are available.
Golfing visitors are welcome.
Secretary: Mr. W.N. Donaldson
-
Tel: (01330) 822365.
Professional Mr. C. Dernie -
Tel: (01330) 822447.

Stonehaven

Stonehaven Golf Club
Cowie, Stonehaven
AB39 3RH.
Tel: (01569) 762124.
18 holes, length of course
4669m/5103 yds.
SSS 65
Charges: On Application.
For advance reservations Tel:
(01569) 762124.
A practice area, catering &
full licensing facilities are
available.
Visitors are welcome Monday
to Friday. Late afternoon and
evening on Saturday and all
day Sunday.
Secretary: Mr. W.A. Donald -
Tel: (01569) 762124.

Torphins

Torphins Golf Club
Torphins.
Tel: (01339) 882115.
9 holes, length of course
4684 yds.
SSS 64
Charges: On Application.
Members evening from 5pm
Tuesdays.
Secretary: Mr. S. MacGregor -
Tel: (01339) 882402.

KINROSS-SHIRE
Kinnesswood
Bishopshire Golf Course
Kinnesswood.
Tel: (01592) 780203.
(Further details on applica-
tion).

Kinross
Green Hotel Golf Courses
Green Hotel.
Tel: (01577) 863407.
Red Course - 18 holes, length
of course 5717m/6256 yds.
SSS 73
Blue Course- 18 holes, length
of course 5888m/6438 yds.
SSS 71
Charges: On Application.
For advance reservation Tel:
Green Hotel.
Caddy cars and catering
facilities are available.
Secretary: M. Smith.

Milnathort

Milnathort Golf Club Ltd
South Street, Milnathort.
Tel: (01577) 864069.
9 holes, length of course
5702 yds.
SSS 68
Charges: £12 daily, £9 per
round
(weekdays), £12 round, £17
daily
(weekends).
For advance reservations Tel:
(01577) 864069.
A practice area is available.
Catering facilities are only
available with prior booking.
Visitors are welcome all week.
Captain:J. Donaldson -
Tel: (01383) 830985.

KIRKCUDBRIGHT-SHIRE
Castle Douglas

Castle Douglas Golf Course
Abercromby Road,
Castle Douglas.
Tel: (01556) 502801.
9 holes, length of course
5408 yds.
SSS 66
Charges: On Application.
Visitors are welcome without
reservation.
Secretary: A.D. Millar -
Tel: (01556) 502099.

Dalbeattie
Colvend Golf Club
Sandyhills, Colvend,
by Dalbeattie.
Tel: (01556) 630398.
18 holes, length of course
4716 yds. 18 holes 1997.
SSS 67
Charges: £15 daily, juniors
£8, except Sat/Sun.
Catering facilities are
available.
Visitors are welcome - (Apr-
Sept course closed: Tues. from
4pm. Thurs from 5.30pm).
Secretary:
Mr. J.B. Henderson,
9 Glenshalloch Road,
Dalbeattie.
Tel: (01556) 610878.

Dalbeattie Golf Club
Dalbeattie.
Tel: (01556) 611421.
(Further details on
application).

Gatehouse of Fleet

Gatehouse Golf Club
Gatehouse of Fleet.
Tel: (01557) 840239.
9 holes, length of course
2398 yds.
Par 66
SSS 64
Visitors welcome all week.
Restrictions Sunday mornings.
Charges: £10 round. £10 day.
Administrator: Mr. K. Cooper -
Tel: (01644) 450260.

Kirkcudbright
Kirkcudbright Golf Club
Stirling Crescent,
Kirkcudbright DG6 4EZ.
Tel: (01557) 330314.
18 holes, length of course
5121m/5739 yds.
SSS 69
Charges: On Application.
Phone for advance
reservations.
Visitors are welcome all week.
Secretary: N. Russell -
Tel: (01557) 330314.

New Galloway

New Galloway Golf Club
New Galloway
DG7 3RN.
9 holes, length of course
2313m/2529 yds.
SSS 65
Charges: On Application.
Visitors are welcome all week.
Secretary: Mr. A. R. Brown -
Tel: (01644) 430455.

LANARKSHIRE
Airdrie

Airdrie Golf Club
Glenmavis Road,
Airdrie ML6 0PQ.
Tel: (01236) 762195.
(Further details on applica-
tion).

Easter Moffat Golf Club
Mansion House, Plains.
Tel: (01236) 842878.
18 holes, length of course
5690m/6222 yds.
SSS 70
Charges: £15 round, £20 daily.
For advance reservations Tel:
(01236) 842878.
A practice area is available.
Visitors are welcome Mon to
Fri
Secretary: Mr. J.G. Timmons -
Tel: (01236) 761440.
Professional: Mr. B. Dunbar.

Biggar

Tel: (01698) 852052.

*Biggar Golf Club
The Park,
Broughton Road,
Biggar ML12 6HA.
Tel: (01899) 220618.
18 holes, length of course
5416 yds.
SSS 66
Par 67
Charges: Weekday £7.25 per
round, weekend £8.50, Jnrs &
OAP's weekdays £3.60, week-
ends £4.25 round.
Daily: Weekdays day ticket
£11,
weekends and Bank holidays
£14. Jnrs &
OAP's £4.50 and £8
Single round tickets available
after 4pm daily.
For advance reservations Tel:
(01899) 220319.
Caddy cars and catering
facilities are available.
Visitors are welcome all week.
Secretary: W.S. Turnbull -
Tel: (01899) 220566.

Leadhills Golf Course
Leadhills, Biggar,
Lanarkshire.
Tel: (01899) 274222.
9 holes, length of course
4150m.
SSS 62
Charges: On Application.
Visitors are welcome all week.
Secretary: Mr. Harry Shaw -
Tel: (01899) 274222.

Bothwell

Bothwell Castle Golf Club
Blantyre Road,
Bothwell, Glasgow G71 8PJ..
Tel: (01698) 853177.
18 holes, length of course
5705m/6240 yds.
SSS 70
Charges: On Application.
For advance reservations Tel:
(01698) 852052.
A practice area, caddy cars
and catering facilities are
available.
Visitors are welcome Mon-Fri
Secretary: D.A. McNaught -
Tel: (01698) 817673.
Professional: Mr. A. McCloskey

Cambuslang
Cambuslang Golf Club
Westburn, Cambuslang.
Tel: 0141-641 3130.
9 holes, length of course
6146 yds.
SSS 69
Visitors welcome when
accompanied by member.
Secretary: William Lilly -
Tel: 0141-641 1498.

Carluke

Carluke Golf Club
Mauldslie Road, Hallcraig,
Carluke ML8 5HG.
Tel: (01555) 771070.
18 holes, length of course
5308m/5805 yds.
SSS 68
Charges: On Application.
Advance reservations must be
made in writing to secretary.
A practice area and catering
facilities are available.
Visitors are welcome all week
until 4pm, except Sat/Sun &
public holidays.
Secretary: D. Black -
Tel: (01555) 770574.
Professional: R. Forrest -
Tel: (01555) 751053.

Carnwath

Carnwath Golf Course
Main Street, Carnwath ML11
8YX.
Tel: (01555) 840251.
(Further details on
application).

Coatbridge

*Coatbridge Golf Club
Townhead Road, Coatbridge.
Tel: (01236) 428975.
18 holes, length of course
5877 yds.
SSS 68
Charges: On Application.
For advance reservations Tel:
(01236) 421492.
A practice area, caddy cars
and catering facilities are
available.
Visitors are welcome at all

times, except 1st Saturday of
month.
Secretary: O. Dolan -
Tel: (01236) 426811.

Drumpellier Golf Club
Drumpellier Avenue,
Coatbridge ML5 1RX.
Tel: (01236) 424139.
Fax: (01236) 428723.
A practice area, caddy cars
and catering facilities are
available.
Visitors are welcome
Mon, Tues, Wed, Thur, Fri.
Secretary: Mr. William
Brownlie -
Tel: (01236) 423065.
Professional: Mr. D. Ross -
Tel: (01236) 432971.

East Kilbride

East Kilbride Golf Club
Nerston,
East Kilbride G74 4PF.
Tel: (01355) 247728.
18 holes, length of course
6419 yds
SSS 71
Charges: £20 round, £30 daily.
Visiting parties welcome
weekdays on application to
the Secretary.
Weekends, no visitors unless
accompanied by a member.
Secretary: W.G. Gray.
Professional: Willie Walker -
Playfair Golf Ltd.

*Torrance House Golf Club
Strathaven Road,
East Kilbride G75 0QZ.
Tel: (013552) 49720.
18 holes, length of course
6415 yds.
SSS 71
Charges: On Application.
For advance reservations Tel:
(012552) 48638.
Caddy cars, practice area and
catering facilities are
available.
Visitors are welcome all week
by arrangement with:
Recreation Manager (Golf),
Leisure Services Department,
East Kilbride District Council,
Civic Centre, East Kilbride.
Tel: (013552) 71296.
Professional: J. Dunlop -
Tel: (013552) 71296.

Glasgow

***Alexandra Golf Course**
Alexandra Park,
Sannox Gardens, Dennistoun,
Glasgow.
Tel: 0141-556 1294.
9 holes, length of course
2008 yds.
Charges: On Application.
Advance bookings welcome.
A practice and catering area
are available.
Visitors are welcome at all
times.
Secretary: G. Campbell.

Bellshill Golf Club
Orbiston, Bellshill ML4 2RZ.
Tel: (01698) 745124.
18 holes, length of course 5900
yds.
SSS 69
Charges:£25 daily.
Advance reservations Tel:
(01698) 745124.
Catering facilities available.
Visitors welcome except Sats.
Secretary: J. Chapman -
Tel - (01698) 745124.

Bishopbriggs Golf Club
Brackenbrae Road,
Bishopbriggs,
Glasgow G64 2DX.
Tel: 0141-772 1810.
18 holes, length of course
6041 yds.
SSS 69.
Charges: On application.
Catering facilities are
available.
Parties are welcome with
reservation, Tues & Thurs
only (apply to secretary at
least one month in advance).
Secretary: James J. Quin -
Tel: 0141-772 8938.

Cawder Golf Club
Cadder Road,
Bishopbriggs.
2 x 18 holes, length of courses:
Cawder 5711m/6244 yds,
Keir 5373m/5885 yds.
SSS 71 & 68
Charges: £25 daily.
For advance reservations Tel:
0141-772 5167.
A practice area, caddy cars
and catering facilities are
available.

Visitors are welcome Monday
to Friday.
Secretary: G.T. Stoddart -
Tel: 0141-772 5167.
Professional: K. Stevely -
Tel: 0141-772 7102.

Cowglen Golf Club
301 Barrhead Road,
Glasgow G43.
Tel: 0141-632 0556.
(Further details on
application).

Crow Wood Golf Club
Garnkirk Estate,
Muirhead,
Chryston G69 9JF.
Tel: 0141-779 2011.
18 hole, length of course 6261
yds.
SSS 71
Par71
Visitors Mon-Fri. (Prior notice
required).
Charges: £20 round. £28 two
rounds.
Packages to include food.
Secretary: I. McInnes -
Tel: 0141-779 4954.
Professional: B. Moffat-
Tel: 0141-779 1943.

*Deaconsbank Golf Course
Rouken Glen Golf Centre,
Stewarton Road,
(Junction A726)
Thornliebank,
Giffnock G46 7UZ.
Tel: 0141-638 7044
or 0141-620 0826.
18 holes, length of course
4800 yds.
SSS 63
(Par 64).
Charges: Mon-Fri £7.75,
Sat/Sun £8.50 per round. Day
ticket
£14.25 & £16.50
Catering facilities are
available.
15 bay floodlit driving range,
shop facilities and hiring of
clubs, etc.
Visitors are welcome.
Secretary: Christine Cosh.

Dougalston Golf Club
Strathblane Road, Milngavie,
Glasgow G62 8HJ.
Tel: 0141-956-5750.
18 holes, length of course BT

6354 - FT 5959 yds.
SSS BT 72 FT 70
Charges: £12 round.
Advance reservations Tel:
0141-956 5750.
Practice area. caddy cars and
catering facilities available.
Visitors welcome Mon-Fri.
Secretary: Ian Glen Muir -
Tel: 0141-956 5750.

Haggs Castle Golf Club
70 Dumbreck Road,
Glasgow G41 4SN.
Tel: 0141-427 1157.
18 holes, length of course
6464 yds.
SSS 71
Charges: £27 round, £38 daily.
For advance reservations Tel:
0141-427 1157.
A practice area, caddy cars
and catering facilities are
available.
Visitors must be introduced by
a member. Parties only on
Wednesdays.
Secretary: Ian Harvey -
Tel: 0141-427 1157.
Professional: J. McAlister -
Tel: 0141-427 3355.

*Kings Park Golf Course
Croft Park Avenue,
Glasgow.
9 holes.
Charges: On Application.
(For further information
contact the Golf Manager on
0141-630 1597).

*Knightswood Golf Course
Lincoln Avenue,
Glasgow G13.
Tel: 0141-959 6358
9 holes.
Charges: On Application.
(Further details on
application).
Secretary: J. Dean -
Tel: 0141-954 6495.

*Lethamhill Golf Course
Hogganfield Loch,
Cumbernauld Road,
Glasgow G33 1AH.
Tel: 0141-770 6220.
18 holes.
Charges: On Application.
(Further details on
application).

*Linn Park Golf Course
Simshill Road,
Glasgow G44 5TA.
Tel: 0141-637 5871.
18 holes.
Charges: On Application.
For advance reservations Tel:
0141-637 5871.

*Littlehill Golf Course
Auchinairn Road,
Glasgow G64 1OT.
Tel: 0141-772 1916.
18 holes.
Charges: On Application.

Mount Ellen Golf Club
Johnstone House,
Johnstone Road, Gartcosh.
Tel: (01236) 872277.
18 holes, length of course
5525 yds.
SSS 67
Charges: £14 round, £22 daily.
Package deal: £32.
Visitors welcome on weekdays
only.
For advance reservations Tel:
(01236) 872277.
Catering facilities are
available.
Secretary: J. Docherty..

Pollok Golf Club
90 Barrhead Road,
Glasgow G43 1BG.
18 holes, length of course 6257
yds.
SSS 70
Secretary: Tel: 0141-632 4351
Fax: 0141-649 1398.
Clubmaster: 0141-632 1080.
(Further details on
application).

*Ruchill Golf Course
Bilsland Drive,
Glasgow G22.
9 holes.
Charges: On Application.
For further information
contact the Golf Manager
on 0141-554 8274.

The Williamwood Golf Club
690 Clarkston Road,
Glasgow G44 3YR.
Tel: 0141-637 1783.
18 holes, length of course
5878 yds.
SSS 69
Charges: On application.

Visitors are welcome by
arrangement and when intro-
duced by, and playing with
members.
Secretary: P. Laing -
Tel: 0141-637 1783.
Professional: J. McTear -
Tel: 0141-637 2715.

Hamilton

Hamilton Golf Club
Riccarton, Ferniegair,
by Hamilton.
Tel: (01698) 282872.
(Further details on
application).

*Strathclyde Park Golf Club
Motehill, Hamilton
Tel: (01698) 429350.
9 holes, length of course
3147 yds.
SSS 70
Charges: On Application.
For advance reservations:
same day booking only - lines
open 8.45am - Tel: (01698)
429350.
A practice area and catering
facilities are available.
Visitors are welcome all week.
Secretary: Kevin Will -
Tel: (01324) 557968.
Professional:W. Walker -
Tel: (01698) 285511.

Lanark

Lanark Golf Club
The Moor,
Whitelees Road, Lanark.
Tel: (01555) 663219.
18 hole and 9 hole, length of
course 6423 yds.
SSS 71 (18 hole)
Charges: On Application.
For advance reservations -
Tel: (01555) 662349.
A practice area, caddy cars
and catering facilities are
available (Caddies if
requested).
Visitors are welcome Monday
to Thursday.
Secretary: G.H. Cuthill -
Tel: (01555) 663219.
Professional:A. White -
Tel: (01555) 661456.

Larkhall

*Larkhall Golf Course
Burnhead Road, Larkhall.
Tel: (01698) 889597.
(Further details on
application).

Lenzie

Lenzie Golf Club
19 Crosshill Road,
Lenzie G66.
Tel: 0141-776 1535.
18 holes, length of course 5984.
SSS 69
Charges: £16 round, £24 daily.
Weekly on application.
For advance reservations Tel:
0141-776 6020.
Practice area, caddy cars and
catering facilities available.
Visitors welcome except week-
ends.
Secretary: Scott M. Davidson -
Tel: 0141-776 6020.
Professional: Jim McCallum -
Tel: 0141-777 7748.

Lesmahagow

*Hollandbush Golf Club
Acretophead, Lesmahagow.
Tel: (01555) 893484.
18 holes, length of course
6218 tds.
SSS 70
Par 71
Practice area and catering
facilities available.
Visitors welcome.
Secretary: J. Hamilton.
Professional: I. Rae -
Tel: (01555) 893643.

Motherwell

Colville Park Golf Club
Jerviston Estate,
Merry Street, Motherwell.
Tel: (01698) 263017.
18 holes, length of course
5724m/6265 yds.
SSS 70 (par 71)
Charges: On Application.
For advance reservations Tel:
(01698) 263017.
A practice area and catering
facilities are available.

Visitors are welcome by prior arrangement Monday to Friday.
Secretary: Scott Connacher - Tel: (01698) 265378 (after 5pm).

Rigside

Douglas Water Golf Club
Ayr Road, Rigside.
Tel: (01555) 880361.
9 holes, length of course 2945m.
SSS 69
Charges: £6 (Mon-Fri) day ticket,
£8 Sun day ticket.
Please write for advance reservations.
A practice area is available, light refreshments are available at the weekend.
Visitors are welcome all week.
No visitors on Saturdays due to competition.
Secretary: Mr. R. Paterson.

Rutherglen

Blairbeth Golf Club
Fernbra Avenue,
Rutherglen G73 4SF.
Tel: 0141-634 3355.
(Further details on application).

Cathkin Braes Golf Club
Cathkin Road,
Rutherglen, Glasgow G73 4SE.
Tel: 0141-634 6605.
18 holes, length of course 6208 yds.
SSS 71
Charges: On Application.
For advance reservations Tel: 0141-634 6605.
Caddy cars, practice area and catering facilities are available.
Visitors are welcome Mon to Fri.
Secretary: H. Millar - Tel: 0141-634 6605.
Professional: S. Bree - Tel: 0141-634 0650.

Shotts

Blairhead Golf Course
Shotts Golf Club
Blairhead, Shotts.
Tel: (01501) 820431.
Charges: On Application.
Visitors are welcome weekdays.
(Further details on application).

Strathaven

Strathaven Golf Club
Overton Avenue,
Glasgow Road, Strathaven.
Tel: (01357) 520539.
18 holes, length of course 5696m/6226 yds.
SSS 70
Charges: £20 round, £30 daily (1995).
For advance reservations Tel: (01357) 520539
A practice area, caddy cars and catering facilities are available.
Secretary: Mr. A.W. Wallace - Tel: (01357) 520421.
Professional: Mr. M. McCrorie - Tel: (01357) 521812.

Uddingston

Calderbraes Golf Club
57 Roundknowe Road, Uddingston.
Tel: (01698) 813425.
(Further details on application).

Wishaw

Wishaw Golf Club
55 Cleland Road, Wishaw.
Tel: (01698) 372869.
18 holes, length of course 6073 yds.
SSS 69
Charges: On Application.
A practice area, caddy cars and catering facilities are available.
Secretary: J.M. Mitchell.
Professional: J. Campbell.

LOTHIANS

Aberlady
Luffness New Golf Club
The Clubhouse,
Aberlady EH32 0QA.
Tel: (01620) 843336.
18 holes, length of course 6122 yds.
SSS 70
Charges: On application.
For advance reservations - Tel: (01620) 843336.
A practice area and catering facilities are available.
Visitors are welcome weekdays by arrangement.
Secretary: Lt. Col. J.G. Tedford - Tel: (01620) 843336.
Clubmaster: Tel: (01620) 843376.

Bathgate

Bathgate Golf Course
Edinburgh Road,
Bathgate EH48 1BA.
Tel: (01506) 652232.
18 holes, length of course 6325 yds.
SSS 70
Charges: £20 daily (Mon-Fri), £30 (Sat/Sun).
For advance reservations Tel: (01506) 630505 (8.00-3pm).
A practice area, caddy cars, buggies and catering facilities are available.
Secretary: Allan Osborne - Tel: (01506) 630505.
Professional: Sandy Strachan - Tel: (01506) 630553.

Bo'ness

West Lothian Golf Club
Airngath Hill,
by Linlithgow.
Tel: (01506) 826030.
18 holes, length of course 6578 yds.
SSS 70
Charges: On Application.
For advance reservations Tel: Neil Robertson -Tel: (01506) 825060.

Caddy cars, practice area and catering facilities are available. Visitors are welcome mid-week at all times.Weekend by arrangement.
Secretary: A.E. O'Neill - Tel: (01506) 326030.

Bonnyrigg

Broomieknowe Golf Club
36 Golf Course Road, Bonnyrigg EH19 2HZ.
Tel: 0131-663 9317.
Fax: 0131-663 2152 (Club).
18 holes, length of course 6150 yds.
SSS 69
Charges: £17 round, £25 daily.
Sat/Sun £20 round 1 round only.
For advance reservations Tel: 0131-663 9317.
A practice area, caddy cars and catering facilities are available.
Visiting Parties are welcome Mon-Fri
Secretary: J. G. White - Tel: 0131-663 9317.
Professional: Mr. M. Patchett - Tel: 0131-660 2035.

Broxburn

Niddry Castle Golf Club
Castle Road, Winchburgh, Broxburn EH52 6RQ.
Tel: (01506) 891097.
9 holes, length of course 5514 yds.
SSS 67
Charges: £12 round, £16 week-end.
For advance reservations Tel; (01506) 891097.
Catering facilities available.
Visitors welcome Mon-Fir. Weekend by arrangement.
SDecretary: M. Walker - Tel: (01506) 891097.

Dalkeith

Newbattle Golf Club Ltd
Abbey Road, Dalkeith, Midlothian.
Tel: 0131-663 2123.
18 holes, length of course 5498m/6012 yds.
SSS 70

Charges: £16 round, £24 daily.
For advance reservations Tel: 0131-660 1631 or secretary.
A practice area, caddy cars and catering facilities are available.
Visitors are welcome all week, except weekends and public holidays.
Secretary: Mr. H.G. Stanners - Tel: 0131-663 1819.

Dunbar

Dunbar Golf Club
East Links, Dunbar EH42 1LT.
Tel: (01368) 862317.
18 holes, length of course 5874m/6426 yds.
SSS 71
Charges: daily - £30 weekdays. £40 weekends.
For advance reservations Tel: (01368) 862317.
A practice area, caddies (if reserved) and catering facilities are available.
Visitors are welcome all week, after 9.30 am (except Thurs).
Secretary: Liz Thom - Tel: (01368) 862317.
Professional: Mr. D. Small - Tel: (01368) 862086.

*Winterfield Golf Club
North Road, Dunbar.
Tel: (01368) 862280.
18 holes.
SSS 65
Charges: On application.
For advance reservations Tel: (01368) 863562.
Caddy cars and catering facilities are available.
Secretary: Mr. M. O'Donnell - Tel: (01368) 862564.
Professional: Mr. K. Phillips - Tel: (01368) 863562.

Edinburgh

Baberton Golf Club
Baberton Avenue, Juniper Green
EH14 5DU.
Tel: 0131-453 3361.
18 holes, length of course 6123 yds.
SSS 70
Charges: £18.50 round, £28.50

daily.
Visitors are welcome Mon-Fri. Catering facilities available by arrangement.
Secretary: E.W. Horberry - Tel: 0131-453 4911.
Professional: K. Kelly - Tel: 0131-453 3555.

*Braid Hills Golf Course
Braid Hills Approach, Edinburgh EH10 6FY.
Tel: 0131-447 6666.
(Further details on application).

The Bruntsfield Links
Golfing Society
32 Barnton Avenue, Davidsons Mains, Edinburgh EH4 6JH.
Tel: 0131-336 2006.
18 holes, length of course 6407 yds
SSS 71
Charges: On application.
For advance reservations Tel: 0131-336 1479 or 0131-336 4050.
Catering facilities are available.
Secretary: CDR. D.M. Sandford - Tel: 0131-336 1479.
Professional: Brian MacKenzie -Tel: 0131-336 4050.

*Carrick Knowe Golf Club
27 Glen Devon Park, Edinburgh.
Tel: 0131-337 2217.
(Further details on application)

Craigentinny Golf Course
Craigentinny Avenue, Edinburgh.
Tel: 0131-554 7501.
(Further details on application).

Craigmillar Park Golf Club
1 Observatory Road, Edinburgh EH9 3HG.
Tel: 0131-667 0047.
18 holes, length of course 5851 yds
SSS 69
Charges: £17.50 round, £25.50 daily.
For advance reservations -

Tel: 0131-667 0047.
Caddy cars, practice area and catering facilities are available.
Visitors are welcome on weekdays before 3.30pm only (not weekends).
Secretary: T. Lawson -
Tel: 0131-667 0047.
Professional: B. McGhee -
Tel: 0131-667 2850

Duddingston Golf Club
Duddingston Road West,
Edinburgh.
Tel: 0131-661 7688.
18 holes, length of course 6420 yds.
SSS 71
Charges: Visitors (Mon-Fri) - £26 round, £34 daily.
Societies - £22 round, £28 daily (Tues & Thurs only).
For advance reservations Tel: 0131-661 7688.
A practice area, caddy cars and catering facilities are available.
Secretary: J.C. Small -
Tel: 0131-661 7688.
Professional: Mr. A. McLean -
Tel: 0131-661 4301.

Kingsknowe Golf Club Ltd
326 Lanark Road,
Edinburgh
EH14 2JD.
Tel: 0131-441 1144.
18 holes, length of course 5469m/5979 yds.
SSS 69
Charges: On Application.
For advance reservations Tel: 0131-441 4030.
A practice area, caddy cars and catering facilities are available.
Visitors are welcome.
Secretary: R. Wallace -
Tel: 0131-441 1145.
Professional: A. Marshall -
Tel: 0131-441 4030.

Liberton Golf Club
297 Gilmerton Road,
Edinburgh EH16 5UJ.
Tel: 0131-664 3009.
18 holes, length of course 5299 yds.
SSS 66
Charges: On Application.
For advance reservations Tel:

0131-664 1056.
A practice area and catering facilities are available.
Visitors are welcome all week - Sat & Sun after 1.30pm only.
Secretary: A.J. R. Poole -
Tel: 0131-664 3009.
Professional: Iain Seath -
Tel: 0131-664 1056.

Lothianburn Golf Club
106a Biggar Road,
Edinburgh EH10 7DU.
Tel: 0131-445 2206.
Visitors welcome.
Secretary/Treasurer: W.F.A. Jardine - Tel: 0131-445 5067.
Professional: Kurt Mungall -
Tel: 0131-445 2288.
(Further details on application).

Merchants of Edinburgh Golf Club
10 Craighill Gardens,
Edinburgh EH10 5PY.
Tel: 0131-447 1219.
18 holes, length of course 4889 yds.
SSS 64
Charges: £15 daily (no round ticket).
For advance reservations Tel: 0131-447 1219.
Catering facilities are available by arrangement.
Visiting clubs welcome Monday to Friday by request to the Secretary.
Secretary: I.L. Crichton -
Tel: 0131-447 2814.
Professional: Neil M. Colquhoun -
Tel: 0131-447 8709.

Mortonhall Golf Club
231 Braid Road, EH10 6PB.
Tel: 0131-447 2411.
18 holes, length of course 5987m/6548 yds.
SSS 72
Charges: On application.
Catering facilities available.
Visitors are welcome with introduction.
Secretary: Mrs. C.D. Morrison -
Tel: 0131-447 6974.
Professional: D. Horn -
Tel: 0131-447 5185.

*Portobello Golf Club
Stanley Street, Edinburgh

EH15.
Tel: 0131-669 4361.
9 holes, length of course 2167m/2400 yds.
SSS 32
Charges: On Application.
For advance reservations Tel: 0131-669 4361.
Visitors are welcome all week.
Secretary: Mr. Alistair Cook.

Prestonfield Golf Club (Private)
6 Priestfield Road North,
Edinburgh.
Tel: 0131-667 1273.
18 holes, length of course 5685m/6216 yds.
SSS 70
Charges: On application.
For advance reservations Tel: 0131-667 8597.
A practice area, caddy cars and catering facilities are available.
Secretary: Mr. A. Robertson.
Professional: G. MacDonald.

Ratho Park Golf Club
Ratho, Newbridge,
Midlothian EH28 8NX.
Tel: 0131-333 2566.
18 holes, length of course 5398m/5900 yds.
SSS 68
Charges: £25 round, £35 daily, £35 weekend.
For advance reservations Tel: 0131-333 1406.
A practice area, caddy cars and catering facilities are available.
Visiting parties are welcome Tues, Wed and Thur.
Secretary: J.S. Yates -
Tel: 0131-333 1752.
Professional: Mr. A. Pate -
Tel: 0131-333 1406.

Ravelston Golf Club
24 Ravelston Dykes Road,
Edinburgh EH4 5NZ.
Tel: 0131-315 2486.
9 holes, length of course 4754m/5200 yds.
SSS 65 (men)
SSS 69 (ladies)
Charges: On Application.
Visitors are welcome (Mon.-Fri.).
Secretary: Mr. Stuart Houston

The Royal Burgess Golfing Society of Edinburgh
181 Whitehouse Road,
Edinburgh EH4 6BY.
Tel: 0131-339 2075.
18 holes, length of course
6494 yds.
SSS 71
Charges: On application
For advance reservations Tel:
0131-339 2075.
Trolley and catering facilities
are available.
Visitors/parties are welcome
Mon-Fri.
Secretary: John P. Audis -
Tel: 0131-339 2075.
Professional: George Yuille -
Tel: 0131-339 6474.

*Silverknowes Golf Club (Private)
Silverknowes Parkway,
Edinburgh EH4 5ET.
Tel: 0131-336 5359.
(further details on
application).

Swanston Golf Club
111 Swanston Road,
Edinburgh EH10 7DS.
Tel: 0131-445 2239.
18 holes, length of course
5024 yds.
SSS 66
Charges: On Application.
For advance reservations Tel:
0131-445 4002 (Prof.).
Catering facilities are
available.
Visitors are welcome
9am-4pm Mon-Fri.
Secretary: John Allan -
Tel: 0131-445 2239.
Professional: I. Taylor -
Tel: 0131-445 4002.

Torphin Hill Golf Club
Torphin Road, Edinburgh
EH13 OPL.
Tel: 0131-441 1100.
18 holes, length of course
4597m/5020 yds.
SSS 66
Charges: On Application.
For advance reservations Tel:
0131-441 1100.
Practice area and catering
facilities are available.
Visitors are welcome all week,
except competition days
(phone for details).

Secretary: R. M. Brannan -
Tel: 0131-441 1100.
Professional: Jamie Browne -
Tel: 0131-441 4061.

Turnhouse Golf Club Ltd.
154 Turnhouse Road,
Edinburgh.
Tel: 0131-339 1014.
18 holes, length of course
6121 yds.
SSS 70
Charges: £16 per round,
£24 daily.
For advance reservations Tel:
0131-539 5937.
Caddy cars, practice area and
catering facilities are
available.
Visitors are welcome (only as
a society) Mon-Fri, except on
competition days - usually
Wednesday and Friday.
Secretary: A.B. Hay -
Tel: 0131-539 5937.
Professional: J. Murray -
Tel: 0131-339 7701.

Fauldhouse

Greenburn Golf Club
Greenburn, Bridge Street,
Fauldhouse.
Tel: (01501) 770292.
(further details on
application).

Gifford

Gifford Golf Club
Secretary,
Edinburgh Road,
Gifford EH41 4QN.
Tel: (01620) 810267.
9 and 11 Tees, length of
course 6243 yds.
SSS 70
Charges: £10 round/daily
(Mon-Sun).
A small practice area is
available.
Visitors welcome, except
Tuesdays, Wednesdays &
Saturdays from 4.00pm,
Sundays from 12 noon. Course
closed all day first Sunday
each month- April to
October.
Secretary: P.M. Blyth -
Tel: (01620) 810267.

Gullane

Gullane No. 1 Golf Course
East Lothian EH31 2BB.
Tel: (01620) 842255.
18 holes, length of course
5913m/6466 yds.
SSS 72
Charges: £44 (Mon-Fri),
£55 (Sat/Sun) round.
£65 daily (Mon-Fri).
(1997 rates).
For advance reservations Tel:
(01620) 842255.
Caddy cars, caddies and
catering facilities are available.
Secretary: A.J.B. Taylor -
Tel: (01620) 842255.
Professional: J. Hume -
Tel:(01620) 843111.

Gullane No. 2 Golf Course
East Lothian EH31 2BB.
Tel: (01620) 842255.
18 holes, length of course
6244 yds.
SSS 70
Charges: £22 round
(Mon-Fri), £27.50 (Sat/Sun).
£32 daily (Mon-Fri), £41.50
(Sat/Sun) (1997 rates).
For advance reservations Tel:
(01620) 842255.
Caddy cars, caddies and
catering facilities are
available.
Secretary: A.J.B. Taylor -
Tel: (01620) 842255.
Professional: J. Hume -
Tel: (01620) 843111.

Gullane No. 3 Golf Course
East Lothian EH31 2BB.
Tel: (01620) 842255.
18 holes, length of course
5252 yds.
SSS 66
Charges: £12 round
(Mon-Fri), £16.50 (Sat/Sun).
£20 daily (Mon-Fri),
£25 (Sat/Sun)
(1997 rates).
For advance reservations Tel:
(01620) 842255.
Caddy cars, caddies and
catering facilities are
available.
Secretary: A.J.B. Taylor -
Tel: (01620) 842255.
Professional: J. Hume -
Tel: (01620) 843111.

The Honourable Company of Edinburgh Golfers

Muirfield, Gullane,
East Lothian EH31 2EG.
Tel: (01620) 842123.
18 holes, length of course
6601 yds.
SSS 73
Charges: £60 round, £80 daily
(1997).
For advance reservations Tel:
(01620) 842123.
Caddies and catering facilities
are available.
Visitors are welcome on
Tuesdays and Thursdays only,
but check with club.
Secretary: Group Captain
J.A. Prideaux - Tel: (01620)
842123.

Haddington

*Haddington Golf Club
Amisfield Park, Haddington.
Tel: (01620) 823627/822727.
18 holes, length of course
5764m/6280 yds.
SSS 70
Charges: £15.50 round (Mon-
Fri), £20.00 (weekends). £23
daily (Mon-Fri), £27 (week-
ends).
For advance reservations Tel:
(01620) 823627.
A practice area, caddy cars
and catering facilities are
available.
Visitors are welcome all week.
Secretary: D.S. Wilson -
Tel: (01620) 823627.
Fax: (01620) 826580.
Professional: J. Sandilands -
Tel: (01620) 822727.

Kilspindie

Kilspindie Golf Club
Aberlady,
EH32 0QD.
Tel: (01875) 870216/870358.
18 holes, length of course
4957m/5410 yds.
SSS 66
Charges: £20 round
(Mon-Fri), £25 (Sat/Sun).
£30 daily (Mon-Fri),
£35 (Sat/Sun).
A practice area, caddy cars
and catering facilities are
available.

Visitors are welcome.
Secretary: R.M. McInnes-
Tel: (01875) 870358.

Kirknewton

Marriott Dalmahoy Hotel and Country Club,
Kirknewton EH27 8EB.
Tel: 0131-333 1845.
Fax: 0131-335 3203.
2 x 18 holes, length of courses
East 6677 yds. West 5185 yds.
SSS 72 (East).
Par 72
SSS 66 (West).
Par 68
Charges: £48 round East,
£32 round West.
One round each course £65.
Catering facilities available.
Trolley, Buggy and Club &
Shoe Hire.
12 bay all weather floodlit
driving range.
Company/Society packages
available on request,
weekdays. (Members and
residents weekends).
Director of Golf & Country
Club: Brian Anderson.
Secretary: Jennifer Bryans.

Lasswade

Melville Golf Course,
Melville Golf Centre,
Lasswade, Midlothian EH18
1AN.
Tel: 0131-663 8038
0131-654 0224 Bookings Only.
Fax: 0131-654 0814.
9 hole Pay and Play
SSS 62
Total length 18 holes
2140m/4530 yds.
Charges: £7 - 9 holes, £12 - 18
holes, Weekday & Concessions.
£9, 9 holes, £16, 18 holes
Weekend.
24 hour advance bookings
Tel: 0131-654 0224 - large
groups well in advance -
Otherwise Play & Play.
22 Bay Floodlit Range. Practice
area and Putting Green. Golf
Shop. P.G.A. tuition.
Equipment Hire - clubs, shoes,
bags, trolleys etc.
Vended drinks - crisps, rolls
etc. Changing room & toilets.

Visitors welcome 7 days all
year. Usual Golf Etiquette
applies.
Large car park, easy access. 3
mins off Edinburgh City
Bypass on A7.
Contact: Mr. & Mrs.
MacFarlane.
Tel: 0131-663 8038.
Course Booking Only -
Tel: 0131-654 0224.
Professional: Garry Carter -
Range/Shop/Tuition -
Tel: 0131-663 8038.

Linlithgow

Linlithgow Golf Club
Braehead, Linlithgow.
Tel: (01506) 842585.
18 holes, length of course
5239m/5729 yds.
SSS 68
Charges: On Application.
For advance reservations Tel:
(01506) 842585.
A practice area, caddy cars
and catering facilities are
available.
Visitors are welcome all week
except Saturdays and
Tuesdays by special
arrangement.
Secretary: Mr. T.B. Thomson -
Tel: (01506) 842585.
Professional: Mr. Derek Smith -
Tel: (01506) 844356.

Livingston

Deer Park Golf & Country Club
Golf Course Road,
Knightsridge West,
Livingston EH54 8PG.
Tel: (01506) 431037.
18 holes, length of course
6688 yds.
SSS 72
Charges: £16 round weekdays,
£22 daily weekdays.
Advance reservations: Tel:
(01506) 431037.
Practice area, caddy cars and
catering facilities available.
Visitors welcome 7 days.
Professional: W. Yule -
Tel: (01506) 431037.

Longniddry

Longniddry Golf Club
Links Road,
Longniddry EH32 ONL.
Tel: (01875) 852141.
Fax: (01875) 853371.
18 holes, length of course
6219 yds.
SSS 70
Charges: £27 per round
weekdays,
£35 day, weekdays. £35 per
round weekends (1997)
For advance reservations Tel:
(01875) 852141.
A practice area, caddy cars
and catering facilities are
available.
Casual visitors may book tee
up to 7 days in advance Tel:
(01875) 852228. Advance
Bookings - greater than 7 days
Tel: (01875) 952241. Handicap
certificate required.
Secretary: N. Robertson -
Tel: (01875) 852141.
Professional: W.J. Gray -
Tel: (01875) 852228.

Musselburgh

The Musselburgh Golf Club
Monktonhall, Musselburgh.
Tel: 0131-665 2005/7055.
18 holes, length of course
6614 yds.
SSS 73
Charges: On application.
Catering facilities are available.
Visitors are welcome with
reservation.
Secretary: G. Finlay/G. Miller
Professional: Mr. F. Mann.

**Musselburgh Old Course
Golf Club**
10 Balcarres Road,
Musselburgh.
Tel: 0131-665 6981.
9 holes, length of course 2690
yds.
SSS 67
Charges: £4.65 round.
For advance reservations Tel:
0131-665 6981.
Practice area and catering
facilities available.
Visitors welcome all week.
Secretary: A. Mitchell.

One of the Oldest Golf Courses
in the World.

North Berwick
Glen Golf Club
East Links,
Tantallon Terrace,
North Berwick EH39 4LE.
Tel: (01620) 892221.
18 holes, length of course
6079 yds.
SSS 69
Charges: On application
Advance booking recommended
Catering facilities available
throughout the year.
Secretary: D.R. Montgomery -
Tel: Starter's box (01620)
892726.
Professional (shop only) R.
Affleck.- Tel: (01620) 894596.

**The North Berwick Golf
Club**
Beach Road, North Berwick.
Tel: (01620) 895040.
18 holes, length of course 6420
yds.
SSS 71
Charges: £30 round, £45 daily.
For advance reservations Tel:
(01620) 892135.
Caddies, practice area, trolley
caddy cars and catering facilities are available.
Visitors welcome all week.
Secretary: A.G. Flood -
Tel: (01620) 895040.
Professional: D. Huish -
Tel: (01620) 893233.

Whitekirk Golf Course
Whitekirk, nr. North Berwick,
East Lothian EH39 5PR.
Tel: (01620) 870300.
18 holes, length of course
6420 yds.
SSS 72
Charges: £16 per round, £25
Day, Mon-Fri. £22 round, £30
day, Sat & Sun.
For advance reservations Tel:
(01620) 870300.
Buggies, practice area, caddy
cars and catering facilities
available.
Visitors Welcome.
Secretary: Chris Patey -
Tel: (01620) 870300.
Professional: Chris Patey -
Tel: (01620) 870300.

Penicuik

Glencorse Golf Club
Milton Bridge,
Penicuik EH26 ORD.
Tel: (01968) 677177.
18 holes, length of course
5205 yds.
SSS 66
Charges: On Application.
For advance reservations Tel:
(01968) 677189.
(Clubs/Societies only).
Caddy cars and catering
facilities are available.
Visitors are welcome on
Mon, Tues, Wed and Thurs.
Secretary: W. Oliver -
Tel: (01968) 677189.
Professional: Mr. C. Jones -
Tel: (01968) 676481.

Prestonpans

**Royal Musselburgh Golf
Club**
Preston Grange House,
Prestonpans EH32 9RP.
Tel: (01875) 810276.
18 holes, length of course
6237 yds.
SSS 70
Charges: £20 (round), £35
(daily) weekdays. £35 (round)
weekends (1996).
Advance reservations in
writing preferable.
Caddy cars, practice area and
catering facilities are
available.
Visitors are welcome
weekdays, except Friday
afternoons.
Management Secretary:
T.H. Hardie -
Tel: (01875) 810276.
Professional: J. Henderson -
Tel: (01875) 810139.

Pumpherston

Pumpherston Golf Club
Drumshoreland Road,
Pumpherston,
Livingston EH53 OLF.
Tel: (01506) 432869.
9 holes, length of course
4969m/5434yds.
SSS 66
Restricted practice area and
catering facilities are available.

Visitors are welcome all week, only with a member.
Secretary: A.H. Docharty - Tel: (01506) 854652.

South Queensferry

Dundas Parks Golf Club
South Queensferry, West Lothian
EH30 9PQ.
Tel: 0131-331 3179
9 holes, length of course 6024 yds.
SSS 70
Charges £10 per round/daily.
For advance reservations Tel: 0131-331 3179.
A practice area is available.
Visitors are welcome (not weekends) by prior arrangement with secretary.
Secretary: Mrs. Joan Pennie - Tel: 0131-331 3179.

Uphall

Uphall Golf Club
Houston Mains, Uphall
EH52 6JT.
7 miles west of Edinburgh Airport.
Tel: (01506) 856404.
18 holes, length of course:
White Tees 5592 yds
SSS 67, Par 69.
Yellow Tees 5272 yds
SSS 66, Par 69
Charges: On Application.
Societies welcome by prior arrangement.
Visitors welcome 7 days, competitions permitting. Advance reservations: Tel: (01506) 855553.
Excellent Clubhouse facilities.
Bar snacks and meals served all day.
Secretary: W.A. Crighton - Tel: (01506) 856404.
Professional: G. Law - Tel:(01506) 855553.

West Calder

Harburn Golf Club
West Calder EH55 8RS.
Tel: (01506) 871131.
18 holes, length of course 5921 yds.
SSS 69

Charges: £16 (Mon-Thurs), £19 (Fri), £21 (Sat/Sun) round; £21 (Mon-Thurs), £26 (Fri), £32 (Sat/Sun) daily. Package deals available for Golf Societies.
For advance reservations Tel: (01506) 871131.
Caddy cars, practice area and catering facilities are available.
Visitors are welcome all week.
Secretary: J. McLinden - Tel: (01506) 871131.
Professional: S. Mills - Tel: (01506) 871582.

Whitburn

*Polkemmet Country Park Golf Club
West Lothian Council, Park Centre, Whitburn
EH47 OAD.
Tel: (01501) 743905.
9 holes, length of course 2969m.
Charges: On application.
15-bay floodlit golf driving range within the park.
Caddy cars, practice area and catering facilities are available.
Visitors are welcome all week.

MORAYSHIRE
Elgin

Elgin Golf Club
Hardhillock,
Birnie Road,
Elgin IV30 3SX.
Tel: (01343) 542338.
18 holes, length of course 5853m/6401 yds.
SSS 71
Charges: Weekdays: £20 round, £25 daily. Weekends: £25 round, £35 daily.
For advance reservations Tel: (01343) 542338.
Caddies (by arrangement), caddy cars, practice area, catering facilities are available.
Visitors are welcome.
Secretary: David F. Black - Tel: (01343) 542338.
Fax: (01343) 542341.
Professional: Ian Rodger - Tel: (01343) 542884.

Fochabers

Garmouth & Kingston Golf Club
Garmouth, Fochabers.
Tel: (01343) 870388.
18 holes, length of course 5395 yds.
SSS 66
Charges: Mon-Fri £11 round, £17 daily. Weekends £16 round, £22 daily. Reduced charges for parties over 12.
For advance reservations Tel: (01343) 870231.
Catering facilities are available.
Visitors are welcome all week.
Secretary: A. Robertson - Tel: (01343) 870231.

Spey Bay Golf Club
Spey Bay Hotel, Spey Bay, Fochabers IV32 7PJ.
Tel: (01343) 820424.
18 holes, length of course 6092 yds.
SSS 69
Charges: On Application.
Caddy cars, practice area, catering facilities and Driving Range on site available.
Visitors and golf outings welcome.
(Enquiries to hotel manager).

Forres

Forres Golf Club
Muiryshade,
Forres IV36 ORD.
Tel: (01309) 672949.
18 holes, length of course 6236 yds.
SSS 70
Charges: £16 round, £22 daily
Weekdays. £18 round, £24 daily
Weekends.
For advance reservations Tel; (01309) 672250
Caddy cars, practice area and catering facilities are available.
Visitors are welcome all week.
Secretary: Margaret Greenway -Tel: (01309) 672949.
Professional: Sandy Aird - Tel: (01309) 672250.

Grantown on Spey

Grantown on Spey Golf Club
Golf Course Road,
Grantown-on-Spey PH26 3HY.
Tel: (01479) 872079
Fax: (01479) 873725.
18 holes, length of course
5710 yds.
SSS 68
Charges: On Application.
For advance reservations Tel:
(01479) 872079.
Caddy cars, practice area,
putting green, shop, bar and
catering facilities are
available.
Visitors are welcome all week.
Secretary: James A. Matheson
-
Tel: (01479) 873154.
Professional: Bill Mitchell -
Tel: (01479) 872398.

Hopeman

Hopeman Golf Club
Hopeman, Elgin,
Morayshire IV30 2TA.
Tel: (01343) 830578.
18 holes, length of course
4817m/5265 yds.
SSS 67
Charges: On Application.
For advance reservations Tel:
(01343) 830578.
A small practice area and
catering facilities are
available.
Visitors are welcome all week.
Secretary: R. Johnston -
Tel: (01343) 830578.

Lossiemouth

Moray Golf Club
Stotfield, Lossiemouth.
Tel: (01343) 812018.
Fax: (01343) 815102.
36 holes.
Charges: On application.
Caddy cars, practice area and
catering facilities are
available.
Visitors are welcome without
reservation.
Secretary: Boyd Russell -
Tel: (01343) 812018.
Professional: A. Thomson -
Tel: (01343) 813330.

Rothes

Rothes Golf Club
Blackhall, Rothes AB38 7AN.
Tel: (01340) 831443.
2 x 9 holes, length of course
4972 yds.
SSS 65
Charges: £8 Mon-Fri, £10
weekends.
Visitors welcome all week.
Secretary: J.P. Tilley -
Tel: (01340) 831277.

NAIRNSHIRE
Nairn

The Nairn Golf Club
Seabank Road, Nairn.
Tel: (01667) 453208.
18 holes, length of course
6745 yds.
SSS 73
Par 72
Charges: £40 round (Mon-Fri).
£50 round (Sat/Sun).
No daily tickets.
For advance reservations Tel:
(01667) 453208.
A practice area, caddies,
caddy cars and catering
facilities are available.
Visitors are welcome all week.
Hosting 37th Walker Cup
in 1999.
Secretary:
Mr. J.G. Somerville -
Tel: (01667) 453208.
Professional: Mr. R. Fyfe -
Tel: (01667) 452787.

Nairn Dunbar Golf Club
Lochloy Road,
Nairn IV12 5AE.
Tel: (01667) 452741.
Fax: (01667) 456897.
18 holes, length of course
6712 yds.
SSS 73
Charges: £23 round, £30 daily
(Mon-Fri). £28 round, £35
daily (Sat/Sun).
A practice area and caddy cars
are available.
Secretary: Mrs. S.J.
MacLennan.
Professional: Brian Mason -
Tel: (01667) 453964.

PEEBLESSHIRE
Innerleithen

Innerleithen Golf Club
Leithen Water.
Tel: (01896) 830951.
9 holes, length of course
6066 yds.
SSS 69
Charges: Mon-Fri £11/£16 per
day. Sat/Sun £13/£19 per day.
Secretary: S.C. Wyse -
Tel: (01896) 830071.
Practice facilities and bar
available. Visitors welcome.

Peebles

Peebles Golf Club
Kirkland Street, Peebles.
Tel: (01721) 720197.
18 holes, length of course
5636m/6160yds.
SSS 70
Charges: £17 round, £23 daily.
A practice area, caddy cars and
catering facilities are available.
Visitors welcome (subject to
tee availability).

West Linton

West Linton Golf Club
West Linton.
Tel: (01968) 660463.
18 holes, length of course
5607m/6132 yds.
SSS 70
Charges: £19 round
(Mon-Fri), £28 (Sat/Sun).
£28 daily (Mon-Fri).
For advance reservations Tel:
(01968) 660256.
A practice area and catering
facilities are available.
Visiting parties welcome Mon-
Fri, casual visitors welcome
also, at weekend after 1pm.
Secretary: G. Scott - Tel:
(01968) 660970 (Office),
(01968) 675843 (Home).

PERTHSHIRE

Aberfeldy

Aberfeldy Golf Club
Taybridge Road, Aberfeldy.
Tel: (01887) 820535.
18 holes, length of course

5100m/5577 yds.
SSS 66
Charges: £22 daily,
£55 weekly. £14 per round.
Caddy cars
and catering facilities are
available all day.
Secretary: C. Henderson -
19 Tayside Place, Aberfeldy.
Tel: (01887) 829509.
Advance bookings at
all times.

Alyth

The Alyth Golf Club
Pitcrocknie,
Alyth PH11 8HF.
Tel: (01828) 632268.
18 holes, length of course
5676m/6205 yds.
SSS 71 (Boxes 70)
Charges: Weekdays £18 round,
£30 daily. Weekends £23 round,
£35 daily.
For advance reservations Tel:
(01828) 632268.
Large practice area, caddy cars
and
catering/bar facilities.
Visitors welcome all week.
Professional: Mr. Tom Melville
Tel: (01828) 632411.

Strathmore Golf Centre
Leroch,
Alyth PH11 8NZ.
Tel: (01828) 633322.
Rannaleroch Golf Course
18 holes, length of course
5933m/6490 yds.
Par 72
Charges: (1997) £14 per round
weekdays, £27 daily,
£18 per round weekend,
£28 daily weekend.

Leitfie Links Golf Course
9 holes, length of course
1572m/1719 yds.
Par 29
Charges: (1996) £5 per round,
£8 for 18 holes.
For advance reservations Tel:
(01828) 633322.
Driving range, caddy cars
and catering facilities avail-
able.
Visitors very welcome all week.
Secretary: Patrick Barron
Tel: (01828) 633322.

Auchterarder

Auchterarder Golf Club
Orchil Road, Auchterarder.
Tel: (01764) 662804.
Fax: (01764) 663711.
18 holes, length of course
5778 yds.
SSS 68
Charges: £17 round, £26 daily,
weekdays. Saturday/Sunday
£23 round, £36 daily.
For advance reservations Tel:
(01764) 662804/663711.
Professional shop and catering
facilities are available.
Secretary: Mr. W.M. Campbell
- Tel: (01764) 662804
(Office hrs. 9am-5pm).
Professional: Gavin Baxter -
Tel: (01764) 663711.

**The Gleneagles Hotel Golf
Courses
King's Course**
The Gleneagles Hotel,
Auchterarder PH3 1NF.
Tel: (01764) 663543.
Fax: (01764) 664440.
18 holes, length of course
6471 yds.
SSS 73
Charges: On application.
Caddies booked in advance are
guaranteed.
Golf Academy and practice
area and
catering facilities are available.
Golf available for residents and
members only.

Monarch's Course
Auchterarder PH3 1NF.
Tel: (01764) 663543.
Fax: (01764) 664440.
18 holes, length of course 5605
7081 yds - at least 4 tees per
hole.
SSS: Blue 74, White 73, Yellow
71, Green 67 (ladies 74), Red
(ladies) 71.
Charges: On application
Golf Academy and practice
area,
carts and catering facilities
are available.
Golf available for residents and
members only.

Queen's Course
Auchterarder PH3 1NF.
Tel: (01764) 663543.
Fax: (01764) 664440.
18 holes, length of course
5965 yds.
SSS 70
Charges: On application
Caddies booked in advance are
guaranteed.
Golf Academy and practice
area and
catering facilities are available.
Golf available for residents and
members only.

Wee Course
Auchterarder PH3 1NF.
Tel: (01764) 663543.
Fax: (01764) 664440.
9 holes, length of course
1481 yds.
Par 27
Charges: On application
Golf Academy and practice
area and catering facilities are
available.
Golf available for residents and
members only.

Blair Atholl

Blair Atholl Golf Course
Golf Course Road,
Blair Atholl.
Tel: (01796) 481 407.
9 holes
SSS 69
Charges: £11 round Mon-Fri;
£14 round Sat/Sun; £50 weekly.
Parties restricted Sundays.
For advance reservations Tel:
(01796) 481407.
A practice area, caddy cars
and catering facilities are
available.
Secretary: J. McGregor.

Blairgowrie

Blairgowrie Golf Club
Lansdowne Course,
Golf Course Road,
Rosemount PH10 6LG.
Tel: (01250) 872622.
18 holes, length of course
6895 yds.
SSS 74

Charges: On application.
Caddies, caddy cars, practice area and catering facilities are available.
Visiting societies are welcome: Mon, Tues & Thurs.
Secretary: J.N. Simpson - Tel: (01250) 872622.
Professional: Gordon Kinnoch - Tel: (01250) 873116.

Rosemount Course
Golf Course Road,
Rosemount,
Blairgowrie PH10 6LG.
Tel: (01250) 872622.
18 holes, length of course 6588 yds.
SSS 73
Charges: On application.
For advance reservations Tel: (01250) 872622.
Caddies, caddy cars, practice area and catering facilities are available.
Visiting societies are welcome Mon, Tues, Thurs.
Secretary: J.N. Simpson - Tel: (01250) 872622.
Professional: Gordon Kinnoch - Tel: (01250) 873116.

Wee Course
Golf Course Road,
Rosemount,
Blairgowrie PH10 6LG.
Tel: (01250) 872622.
9 holes, length of course 4614 yds.
SSS 65
Charges: On application.
Secretary: J.N. Simpson - Tel: (01250) 872622.
Professional: Gordon Kinnoch - Tel: (01250) 873116.

Callander

Callander Golf Club
Aveland Road,
Callander FK17 8EN.
Tel: (01877) 330090.
18 holes, length of course 5125 yds.
Charges: Weekdays £17.50, weekends £22.50 (round).
Weekdays £22.50, weekends £28 (daily).
For advance reservations Tel: Society Bookings (01877) 330090. Fax: (01877) 330062.
Caddies, caddy cars, practice

area and catering facilities are available.
Visitors welcome all days but with
Handicap Certificates or proof of recognised golf club on Wednesdays and Sundays.
Secretary: I.A.C. Scott - Tel: (01877) 330090.
Professional: W. Kelly - Tel: (01877) 330975.

Comrie

Comrie Golf Club
Secretary,
9 Cowden Way,
Comrie PH6 2NW.
Tel: (01764) 670941.
9 holes, length of course 6016 yds.
SSS 70
Charges: £10 daily (£12 weekends and public holidays). £45 weekly.
For advance reservations Tel: (01764) 670055.
A practice area, caddy cars, mobile buggy also available and catering facilities.
Visitors are welcome all week, except Monday and Tuesday evenings from 4.30pm.
Secretary: G.C. Betty.

Crieff

Crieff Golf Club Ltd
Perth Road, Crieff PH7 3LR.
Tel: (01764) 652909.

Ferntower Course:
18 holes, length of course 6402 yds.
SSS 71
Charges: On application.

Dornock Course:
9 holes, length of course 2386 yds.
SSS 63
Charges: On application.
For all reservations Tel: (01764) 652909.
Buggies, caddy cars and catering facilities are available.
Visitors are welcome all week (it is advisable to book well in advance).
Secretary: J.S. Miller -

Tel: (01764) 652397.
Professional: D. Murchie - Tel: (01764) 652909.

Foulford Inn Golf Club
by Crieff PH7 3LN.
Tel: (01764) 652407.
9 holes, length of course 916 yds.
SSS 27
Charges: £3 round, £5 daily.
For advance reservations Tel: (01764) 652407.
Catering facilities available.
Visitors welcome all week.

Dunblane

Dunblane New Golf Club
Perth Road, Dunblane FK15 OLJ.
Tel: (01786) 823711.
18 holes, length of course 5536 yds.
SSS 67
Charges: £18 round (Mon-Fri), £27 day. (Sat/Sun) £27 round.
(Charges subject to revision).
For advance reservations Tel: (01786) 823711.
Caddy cars and catering facilities (by advance order) are available.
Visitors are welcome Monday to Friday.
Secretary: John H. Dunsmore - Tel: (01786) 825281.
Professional: R.M. Jamieson - Tel: (01786) 823711.

Dunkeld

Dunkeld & Birnam Golf Club
Fungarth, Dunkeld.
Tel: (01350) 727524.
9 holes, length of course 5264 yds.
SSS 66
Charges: On application
For advance reservations Tel: (01350) 727564.
Caddy cars and catering facilities are available.
Visitors are welcome all week without reservation.
Secretary: Mrs. W.A. Sinclair - Tel: (01350) 727564.

Dunning

Dunning Golf Club
Rollo Park, Dunning.
Tel: (01764) 684747.
9 holes, length of course
4836 yds.
SSS 63
Charges: On Application.
For Club/society bookings-
Tel: (01764) 684372.
Caddy cars available.
Secretary: Mrs May Ramsey -
Tel: (01764) 684237.

Glenshee (Spittal O')

Dalmunzie Golf Course
Glenshee, Blairgowrie PH10
7QG.
Tel: (01250) 885224
9 holes, length of course
2036 yds.
SSS 60
Charges: £10.00 daily.
Under-14's half price,
under-7's free.
Weekly family ticket £75.
Catering and accommodation
available.

Kenmore

Kenmore Golf Course
Mains of Taymouth,
Kenmore.
Tel: (01887) 830226.
9 holes, length of course
2751m/3026 yds.
18 holes, length of course
5502m/6052 yds.
SSS 69
Charges: On Application.
For advance reservations Tel:
(01887) 830226.
Practice area, caddy cars and
catering facilities are
available.
Parties and visitors welcome.
Secretary: Robin Menzies -
Tel: (01887) 830226.

**Taymouth Castle Golf
Course**
Kenmore, Tayside PH15 2NT.
Tel: (01887) 830228.
Fax: (01887) 830765.
18 holes, length of course
6066 yds.
Mens Medal Tees SSS 69

Yellow Tees SSS 67
Ladies SSS 72
Charges: Weekday £17,
weekend & Bank Hols, £21
(round). £38 daily. Weekdays
£28 (daily).
For advance reservations -
Tel: (01887)
830228.
Caddy cars, a practice area
and catering facilities are
available.
Visitors are welcome all week
with reservations.
Professional: Alex Marshall -
Tel: (01887) 830228.

Killin

Killin Golf Club
Killin Golf Course,
Killin.
Tel: (01567) 820312.
9 holes, length of course
2508yds.
SSS 65
Charges: On Application.
Caddy cars and catering
facilities are available.
Visitors are welcome all week.
Secretary: Mr. J. Greaves -
Tel: (01567) 820705.

Muthill
Muthill Golf Club
Peat Road, Muthill,
Crieff PH5 2AD.
Tel: (01764) 681523.
9 holes, length of course
2350 yds
SSS 63 Men   SSS 69 Ladies
Charges: £12 round 18 holes.
£15 Day Ticket. No increase at
Weekends. Weekly Highland
Ticket available on request.
Party bookings taken. Visitors
welcome all week.
Morning coffee, lunches, high
teas. Golf clubs & trolley hire
available.
For reservations: The
Clubhouse Manager - Tel:
(01764) 681523.

Perth
The Craigie Hill Golf Club
(1982) Ltd.
Cherrybank, Perth.
Tel: (01738) 624377.
18 holes, length of course
5386 yds.

SSS 67
Charges:
£15 round (Mon-Fri).
£20 daily (Mon-Fri).
£25 daily (Sun).
For advance reservations Tel:
(01738) 622644.
A practice area and catering
facilities are available.
Visitors are welcome all week
except Saturdays.
Secretary: David R. Allan -
Tel: (01738) 620829.
Professional: S. Harrier -
Tel: (01738) 622644.

King James VI Golf Club
Moncreiffe Island, Perth.
Tel: (01738) 625170/632460.
18 holes, length of course
5177m/5664 yds.
SSS 68
Charges: £15 round, £22 daily
(Mon-Fri), £28 (Sun) (1997).
For advance reservations Tel:
(01738) 632460.
A practice area, caddy cars
and catering facilities are
available.

Murrayshall Golf Club
Murrayshall Country House
Hotel & Golf Course,
Scone PH2 7PH.
Tel: (01738) 551171.
18 holes, length of course
5901m/6460 yds.
SSS 71
Charges: On application.
For advance reservations Tel:
(01738) 551171.
Caddies, caddy cars, buggies,
practice area and catering
facilities are available.
Visitors are welcome all week.
Professional: Neil MacIntosh -
Tel: (01738) 552784.

*North Inch Golf Club
North Inch (off Hay Street),
Perth.
18 holes, length of course
5178m.
SSS 65
Charges: £5.25 Mon-Fri,
£7 Sat & Sun round.
For advance reservations Tel:
(01738) 636481.
Catering facilities are
available.
Visitors are welcome all week.

Pitlochry

Pitlochry Golf Course Ltd.,
Golf Course Road,
Pitlochry PH16 5Q7.
Tel: (01796) 472792 (bookings).
18 holes, length of course
5811 yds.
SSS 69
Charges: On Application.
Caddy cars, tuition and
catering facilities are
available.
Visitors are welcome all week.
Secretary: D.M. McKenzie.
Professional:
George Hampton -
Tel: (01796) 472792.

St. Fillans

St. Fillans Golf Club
South Lochearn Road,
St. Fillans.
Tel: (01764) 685312.
9 holes, length of course
4812m/5628 yds.
SSS 67
Charges: £10 day
ticket (Mon-Fri); £15 day ticket
(Sat/Sun/Bank hols).
Caddy cars and limited
catering facilities are
available.
Visitors are welcome all week.
Visiting clubs by arrangement.
Secretary: K.W. Foster -
Tel: (01764) 685312/679509

Strathtay

Strathtay Golf Club
Lorne Cottage, Dalguise,
Dunkeld PH8 OJX.
Tel: (01350) 727797.
9 holes, length of course
4082 yds (18 holes).
SSS 63
Charges: On Application.
For advance reservations
Tel: (01350) 727797.
Visitors are welcome all week,
except Sun 12-5 and Mon 6-9.
Secretary: T.D. Lind. (All
Correspondence - Lorne
Cottage, Dalguise, Dunkeld
PH8 OJX. Tel: (01350)
727797.

RENFREWSHIRE
Barrhead

Fereneze Golf Club
Fereneze Avenue,
Barrhead.
Tel: 0141-881 1519
18 holes, length of course
5908yds.
SSS 70
Visiting parties on application
Monday to Friday.
Contact secretary:
A. Johnston, C.A., -
7 Glasgow Road,
Paisley PA1 3QS.
Telephone: 0141-887 4141
Fax: 0141-887 1103.

Bishopton

Erskine Golf Club
Bishopton PA7 5PH.
Tel: (01505) 862302.

Bridge of Weir

**Ranfurly Castle Golf Club
Ltd**
Golf Road, Bridge of Weir.
Tel: (01505) 612609.
18 holes, length of course 6284
yds.
SSS 71
Charges: £25 round, £35 daily.
For advance reservations Tel:
(01505) 612609.
Practice area, caddy cars and
catering facilities available.
Visitors welcome weekdays
only.
Secretary: J. Walker -
Tel: (01505) 612609.
Professional: T. Eckford.

**The Old Course Ranfurly
Golf Club Ltd.,**
Ranfurly Place, Bridge of Weir
PA11.
Tel: (01505) 613214/613612.
18 holes, length of course 6200
yds.
SSS 70
Charges: £20 round, £30 daily.
For advance reservations Tel:
(01505) 613214.
Catering facilities available.
Visitors welcome Tues, Wed &
Thurs.
Secretary: R. Mitchell -
Tel: (01505) 613214.

Caldwell

Caldwell Golf Club Ltd
Uplawmoor G78.
18 holes, length of course
6207 yds.
SSS 70
Charges: On Application.
For advance reservations Tel:
(01505) 850616.
Caddy cars, practice area and
catering facilities are available.
Visitors are welcome Mon-Fri
Secretary: H.I.F. Harper -
Tel: (01505) 850366.
Professional: Stephen Forbes -
Tel: (01505) 850616.

Eaglesham

Bonnyton Golf Club
Eaglesham
G76 OQA.
Tel: (01355) 302781.
18 holes, length of course
6252 yds.
SSS 71
Charges: £27 daily.
Caddy cars, practice area
and catering facilities are
available.
Visitors welcome Monday
to Friday.
Secretary: A. Hughes -
Tel: (01355) 302781.
Professional: K. McWade -
Tel: (01355) 302256.

Elderslie

Elderslie Golf Club
63 Main Road, Elderslie.
Tel: (01505) 322835/323956.
18 holes, length of course
6175 yds.
SSS 70
Charges: £18 round,
£24 daily.
For advance reservations Tel:
(01505) 323956.
A practice area and catering
facilities are available.
PlusP.G.A. professional shop
etc.
Secretary: A. Anderson -
Tel: (01505) 323956.

Gourock

Gourock Golf Club
Cowal View, Gourock PA19
1HD.
Tel: (01475) 631001.
18 holes, length of course
5936m/6512yds.
SSS 73
Charges: On application.
A practice area and catering
facilities are available.
Visitors are welcome Monday
to Friday.
Secretary: Mr. A. D. Taylor -
Tel: (01475) 631001.
Professional: Gavin Coyle -
Tel: (01475) 636834.

Greenock

Greenock Golf Club
Forsyth Street, Greenock
PA16 8RE.
Tel: (01475) 720793.
27 holes, length of course
5838 yds.
SSS 68
Charges: £13 round, £17 daily.
For advance reservations Tel:
(01475) 787236.
A practice area, caddy cars
and catering facilities are
available.
Visitors are welcome Tuesday,
Friday and Sunday.
Secretary: E.J. Black.
Professional: Graham Ross

Cochrane Castle Golf Club
Craigston, Johnstone
PA5 OHF.
Tel: (01505) 320146.
18 holes, length of course
6226 yds.
SSS 70
Charges: £17 round,
£25 daily.
Advance reservations by letter
only.
Caddy cars, a practice area
and catering facilities are
available.
Visitors are welcome Monday
to Friday.
Secretary: J.C. Cowan -
Tel: (01505) 320146.
Professional: Jason J. Boyd
- Tel: (01505) 328465.

**Greenock Whinhill Golf
Club**
Beith Road,
Greenock.
Tel: (01475) 724694.
18 holes, length of course 5504
yds.
SSS 68
Charges: On application.
Visitors welcome all week.
Secretary: Raymond
Kirkpatrick-
Tel: (01475) 724694.

Kilmacolm

Kilmacolm Golf Club
Porterfield Road,
Kilmacolm.
Tel: (01505) 872139.
18 holes, length of course
5890 yds.
SSS 69
Charges: On Application.
Caddy cars, a practice area
and catering facilities are
available.
Visitors are welcome on
weekdays.
Professional: D. Stewart -
Tel: (01505) 872695.

Langbank

The Gleddoch Club
Langbank PA14 6YE.
Tel: (01475) 540711.
Fax: 901475) 540201.
18 holes, length of course
6332 yds.
SSS 71
Charges: £30 for visitors
(day ticket).
For advance reservations Tel:
(01475) 540704.
Buggies,trolleys, practice area,
hire of equipment and catering
facilities are available.
Adjacent to course is Gleddoch
House Hotel.
Visitors are welcome Monday
thru' Friday excluding Bank
Holidays. Golf Day Packages
and Golf Breaks available.
Secretary: Tel: (01475) 540304.
Professional: (01475) 540704.

Lochwinnoch

Lochwinnoch Golf Club
Burnfoot Road, Lochwinnoch.
Tel: (01505) 842153.
Length of course 6243 yds.
SSS 71
Charges: £15 round, £20 daily.
For advance reservations write
to secretary.
A practice area, caddy cars
and catering facilities are
available.
Visitors are welcome Monday
to Friday.
Secretary: Mrs.Wilson -
Tel: (01505) 842153.
Professional: Gerry Reilly -
Tel: (01505) 843029.

Newton Mearns

Cathcart Castle Golf Club
Mearns Road,
Glasgow G76 7YL.
Tel: 0141-638 9449.
18 holes, length of course
5330m/5832 yds.
(Further details on
application).

**The East Renfrewshire
Golf Club**
Pilmuir, Newton Mearns,
Glasgow G7 6RT.
Tel: (01355) 500256.
(Further details on
application).

Eastwood Golf Club
Muirshield, Loganswell,
Newton Mearns,
Glasgow G77 6RX.
Tel: (01355) 500261.
18 holes, length of course
5864 yds.
SSS 68
Charges: £20 round, £30 daily.
(Subject to prior application
and approval).
For advance reservations Tel:
(01355) 500280.
Caddy cars and catering
facilities are available.
Visitors are welcome all week.
Secretary: V.E. Jones -
Tel: (01355) 500280 (a.m. only).
Professional: A. McGinness -
Tel: (01355) 500285.

Paisley

*Barshaw Golf Club
Barshaw Park, Paisley.
Tel: 0141-889 2908.
18 holes, length of course
5703 yds.
SSS 67
Charges: On Application.
Visitors are welcome all week.
Secretary: Mr. W. Collins -
Tel: 0141-884 2533.

The Paisley Golf Club
Braehead, Paisley PA2 8TZ.
Tel: 0141-884 2292.
18 holes, length of course
6466 yds.
SSS 72
Charges: £20 round,
£28 daily. (1997)
Handicap Certificate required.
A practice area and catering
facilities are available.
Secretary: W.J. Cunningham -
Tel: 0141-884 3903.
Professional: G. Stewart -
Tel: 0141-554 4114.

Ralston Golf Club
Strathmore Avenue,
Ralston, Paisley.
Tel: 0141-883 9837.
18 holes.
SSS 69
Charges: On application.
For advance reservations Tel:
0141-883 9837.
Caddy cars and catering facili-
ties available.
Visitors welcome midweek by
prior arrangement.
Secretary: J. Pearson -
Tel: 0141-882 1503.
Professional: John Scott -
Tel: 0141-810 4925.

Port Glasgow

Port Glasgow Golf Club
Devol Road, Port Glasgow.
Tel: (01475) 704181.
18 holes, length of course
5592m/5712 yds.
SSS 68
Charges: On Application.
For advance reservations Tel:
(01475) 704181.
A practice area and catering
facilities are available.
Visitors are welcome

uninvited before 3.55 pm, not
on Saturdays and invited only
Sundays.
Secretary: N.L. Mitchell -
Tel: (01475) 706273.

Renfrew

Renfrew Golf Club
Blythswood Estate,
Inchinnan Road, Renfrew.
Tel: 0141-886 6692.
Fax: 0141-886 1808.
18 holes, length of course
6231m/6818 yds.
SSS 73
Charges: £25 round, £35 daily.
Catering services are
available.
Secretary: I Murchison -
Tel: 0141-886 6692.

ROSS-SHIRE
Alness

Alness Golf Club
Ardross Road, Alness.
Tel: (01349) 883877.
9 holes, length of course
4718 yds.
SSS 63
Par 66
Charges: £8.00 round week-
days,
£10.00 Sat-Sun. Juniors £5 all
week, daily. O.A.P's half price.
For advance reservations Tel:
(01349) 883877.
A practice area and catering
facilities are available.
Visitors are welcome all week.
Secretary: Mrs. B. Taylor - Tel:
(01349) 883877.

Fortrose

**Fortrose & Rosemarkie Golf
Club**
Ness Road East,
Fortrose IV10 8SE.
Tel: (01381) 620529.
18 holes, length of course
5858 yds.
SSS 69
Charges: £16 per round,
£22 daily - Mon-Fri;
£22 per round Sat & Sun, £30
daily. £55 5-day ticket.
£85 10-day ticket.
For advance reservations Tel:

(01381) 620529 (parties only).
A practice area and caddy car
available.
Visitors are welcome all week.
Secretary: Margaret Collier -
Tel: (01381) 620529.

Gairloch

Gairloch Golf Club
Gairloch IV21 2BQ
Tel: (01445) 712407.
9 holes, length of course
(18 holes) 4250 yds.
SSS 63
Charges: On Application.
Caddy cars are available. Club
hire.
Visitors are welcome all week.
Secretary: A. Shinkins -
Tel: 0144 586 346.

Invergordon

Invergordon Golf Club
King George Street,
Invergordon.
Tel: (01349) 852715.
18 holes, length of course 6020
yds.
SSS 69
Charges: £12 round, £15 per
day. Weekly/fortnightly charges
on application.
Practice area available. Clubs,
caddy cars for hire. Bar &
catering facilities are available
May-August except Mondays.
Visitors and Visiting Parties
welcome.
Secretary: N.R. Paterson -
Tel: (01349) 882693.

Lochcarron

Lochcarron Golf Club
Lochcarron, Wester Ross.
Tel: (01520) 722257.
9 holes, length of course
1733 yds.
SSS 60
Charges: £6 (round), £8
(daily), £18 (weekly).
Visitors are welcome all week.
Secretary: G. Weighill -
Tel: (01520) 722257.

Muir of Ord

Muir of Ord Golf Club
Great North Road,
Muir of Ord IV6 7SX.
Tel: (01463) 870825.
18 holes, length of course
5557 yds.
SSS 68
Charges: On Application.
For advance reservations Tel:
(01463) 871311/870825.
A practice area and catering
facilities are available.
Visitors are welcome all week.
Administrator/Manager: Mr. D.
Noble -
Tel: (01463) 870825.
Professional: Mr. G. Vivers -
Tel: (01463) 871311.

Portmahomack

Tarbat Golf Club
Portmahomack.
Tel: (01862) 871236.
(Further details on
application.)

Strathpeffer

Strathpeffer Spa Golf Club
Strathpeffer IV14 9AS.
Tel: (01997) 421219.
18 holes, length of course
4000m/4792 yds.
SSS 64
Charges: £12 round, £16 daily.
Weekly (Mon-Fri) £50. Package
deal with meals. (anyday) £25.
For advance reservations Tel:
(01997) 421219/421011.
A practice area, caddy cars
and catering facilities are
available.
Visitors are welcome all week.
Secretary: Mr. N. Roxburgh -
Tel: (01997) 421396.
Shop: Tel/Fax: (01997) 421011.

Tain

Tain Golf Club
Tain.
Tel: (01862) 892314.
Length of course 6311 yds.
SSS 70
Charges: On application.
For advance reservations Tel:
(01862) 892314.

Full catering facilities are
available.
Visitors are welcome.
Secretary: Mrs. K.D. Ross.

ROXBURGHSHIRE
Hawick

Hawick Golf Club
Vertish Hill, Hawick TD9 0NY.
Tel: (01450) 372293.
18 holes, length of course
5390m/ 5929 yds.
SSS 69
Charges: £18 per round, £24
per day 7 days each week.
For advance reservations Tel:
(01450) 372293.
Caddy cars and catering facili-
ties available.
Visitors welcome all week but
course normally busy Sat.
before 3pm.
Secretary: J. Harley -
Tel: (01450) 374947.

Minto Golf Club
Denholm, Hawick.
Tel: (01450) 870220.
18 holes, length of course
4992m/5460 yds.
SSS 68
Charges: Weekdays £13 per
round, £20 per day. Weekends/
Public holidays, £20 per round,
£27 per day.
For advance reservations Tel:
(01450) 870220.
A practice area, caddy cars
and catering facilities are
available.
Visitors are welcome all week.
Secretary: Dr. Ian Todd -
Tel: (01835) 862611.

Jedburgh

Jedburgh Golf Club
Dunion Road, Jedburgh.
Tel: (01835) 863587.
9 holes, length of course
2746m/5492 yds.
SSS 67
Charges: On Application.
For advance reservations Tel:
(01835) 863587 (Evenings).
Catering facilities are
available.
Visitors are welcome all week.
Secretary: R. Strachan.

Kelso

Kelso Golf Club
Racecourse Road, Kelso.
Tel: (01573) 223009.
(Further details on
application).

Melrose

Melrose Golf Club
The Clubhouse,
Dingleton Road, Melrose.
Tel: (01896) 822855.
9 holes, length of course
5098m/5579yds
SSS 68
Charges: £15 day or round
(7 days)
Visitors welcome excluding
Saturdays.
(Further details on
application).

Newcastleton

Newcastleton Golf Club
Holm Hill,
Newcastleton.
9 holes, length of course
5748m.
SSS 68
Charges: £7 weekdays,
£8 weekends.
For advance reservations Tel:
(01387) 375257.
Visitors are welcome all week.
Secretary: F.J. Ewart -
Tel: (01387) 375257.

St. Boswells

St. Boswells Golf Club
St. Boswells.
Tel: (01835) 823527.
9 holes, length of course
5250 yds.
SSS 65
Charges: Mon-Fri £10.
Sat-Sun £15.
For advance reservations Tel:
(01835) 823527.
Visitors are welcome all week.
Secretary: J.G. Phillips -
Tel: (01835) 823527.

SELKIRKSHIRE
Galashiels

Galashiels Golf Club
Ladhope Recreation Ground,
Galashiels.
Tel: (01896) 753724.
18 holes, length of course
5185 yds.
SSS 66
Charges: £13 Mon-Fri,
£15 Sat & Sun per round. £18
Mon-Fri, £20 Sat & Sun daily.
Booking essential for parties
of 8 or more at weekends.
Tel: (01896) 753724.
A practice area and catering
facilities are available.
Visitors are welcome all week
but booking essential for
w/ends.
Secretary: R. Gass -
Tel: (01896) 755307.

Torwoodlee Golf Club
Edinburgh Road, Galashiels.
Tel: (01896) 752260.
18 holes, length of course
6200 yds.
Charges: £15 round, £20 daily
Mon-Fri.
£20 round, £25 daily weekends.
A practice area, caddy cars
and catering facilities are
available.
Visitors are welcome all week,
except Saturdays to 5.00pm
and Thursdays 1.00-2.00pm
and
4.00-6.00pm.
Secretary: A. Wilson -
Tel: (01896) 752260.

Selkirk

Selkirk Golf Club
Selkirk Hills, Selkirk.
Tel: (01750) 20621.
9 holes, length of course
5636 yds.
Charges: On Application.
Visitors are welcome. Parties
of 8 or more should confirm.
Catering & Bar available on
request.
Secretary: A. M. Wilson -
Tel: (01750) 20907.

STIRLINGSHIRE
Aberfoyle

Aberfoyle Golf Club
Braeval, Aberfoyle.

Tel: (01877) 382493.
18 holes, length of course
4760m/5204 yds.
SSS 66
Charges: On Application.
For advance reservations
Tel: (01877) 382493.
Visitors are welcome all week,
restrictions at weekends.
Secretary: R.D. Steele -
Tel: (01877) 382638.

Balmore

Balmore Golf Club
Balmore, Torrance.
Tel: 0141-332 0392.
18 holes, length of course
5542 yds.
SSS 66
Charges: On Application.
For advance reservations Tel:
0141-332 0392.
A practice area, caddy cars and
catering facilities are available.
Visitors are welcome
Mon-Fri with a member.
Secretary: G.P. Woolard -
Tel: 0141-332 0392.

Bonnybridge

Bonnybridge Golf Club
Larbert Road,
Bonnybridge FK4 1NY.
Tel: (01324) 812822.
9 holes, length of course
6058 yds.
SSS 69
Charges: On Application.
Practice area and catering
facilities are available.
Visitors welcome by
arrangement.
Secretary: C.M.D. Munn -
Tel: (01324) 812822.

Bridge of Allan

Bridge of Allan Golf Club
Sunnylaw, Bridge of Allan,
Stirling.
Tel: (01786) 832332.
9 holes, length of course
4508m/4932yds.
SSS 65
Charges: £8 round,
£12 Sundays.
A practice area is available.
Visitors are welcome all week
except Saturday and during
Sunday competitions.

Secretary: S. Green -
Tel: (01786) 833135.

Drymen

Buchanan Castle Golf Club
Drymen.
Tel: (01360) 660369/07/30.
18 holes, length of course
6086 yds.
SSS 69
Charges: On Application.
For advance reservations Tel:
(01360) 660307.
Visitors are welcome by
arrangement.
Secretary: R. Kinsella -
Tel: (01360) 660307.
Professional: Mr. K. Baxter -
Tel: (01360) 660330.
Strathendrick Golf Club
Drymen
Tel: (01360) 660695.
9 holes, length of course
5116 yds (gents),
4586 yds (ladies).
SSS 65 (gents)
SSS 64 (ladies)
Charges: On application
Visitors are welcome Mon-Fri,
May - Sept, must be accompa-
nied by members at weekends,
restrictions on competition
days.
Secretary: J. Vickers -
Tel: (01360) 660675.

Falkirk

Falkirk Golf Club
Stirling Road,
Camelon, Falkirk.
Tel: (01324) 611061/612219.
18 holes, length of course
6267 yds.
SSS 69
Charges: £15 round, £20 daily.
£30 Sunday.
Advance reservations by
arrangement with starter Tel:
(01324) 612219.
A practice area and catering
facilities are available.
Visitors are welcome Monday
to Friday up to 4.00pm,
(Parties -
Mon/Tues/Thurs/Fri/Sun).
Secretary: J. Elliott -
Tel: (01324) 634118
(home).

*Grangemouth Golf Course
Polmont Hill, By Falkirk.
Tel: (01324) 711500.
(Further details on
application).

Kilsyth

Kilsyth Lennox Golf Club
Tak-Ma-Doon Road,
Kilsyth G65 OHX.
Tel: (01236) 824115.
18 holes, length of course
5912 yds.
SSS 69
Par 70
Charges: On Application.
Catering facilities are
available.
Visitors are welcome all week
with reservation.
Secretary: A.G. Stevenson.

Larbert

Falkirk Tryst Golf Club
86 Burnhead Road,
Stenhousemuir,
Larbert FK5 4BD.
Tel: (01324) 562415.
18 holes, length of course
5533m/6083 yds
SSS 69
Charges: £16 round, £25 daily.
For advance reservations Tel:
(01324) 562054.
Golf trolleys, practice area and
catering facilities are
available.
No unintroduced visitors on
Saturdays/Sundays.
Secretary: R.D. Wallace -
Tel: (01324) 562415/562054.
Professional: Steven
Dunsmore -
Tel: (01324) 562091.

Glenbervie Golf Club
Stirling Road,
Larbert FK5 4SJ.
Tel: (01324) 562605.
18 holes, length of course
6469 yds.
SSS 71
Charges: £30 round, £45 daily.
For advanced reservations
Tel: (01324) 562605 (visiting
parties).
A practice area, caddy cars
and catering facilities are
available.
Visitors are welcome Monday

to Friday.
Secretary: Mrs. M. Purves -
Tel: (01324) 562605.
Professional: Mr. J. Chillas -
Tel: (01324) 562725.

Lennoxtown
Campsie Golf Club
Crow Road,
Lennoxtown G65 7HX.
Tel: (01360) 310244.
18 holes, length of course
5509yds
SSS 68
Par 70
Charges: £12 round Mon-Fri,
£20 per day. £15 round Sat-Sun
after 4pm.
Catering facilities available.
Visitors welcome any time
Mon-Fri, weekends by arrange-
ment.
Secretary: D Barbour -
Tel: (01360) 310244.
Professional: M. Brennan -
Tel: (01360) 310920.

Maddiston
Polmont Golf Club Ltd.
Manuel Rigg, Maddiston,
Falkirk FK2 OLS.
Tel: (01324) 711277.
9 holes, length of course
6603 yds.
SSS 70
Charges: Daily - £7 (Mon-Fri),
£12 Sunday.
Catering facilities are
available.
Visitors are welcome all week,
except after 5pm and
Saturdays.
Secretary: P. Lees -
Tel: (01324) 713811.

Stirling
Stirling Golf Club
Queen's Road,
Stirling FK8 3AA.
Tel: (01786) 473801.
18 holes, length of course
6123 yds.
SSS Medal 71, Front Tee 69.
Charges: £20 round, £30 daily.
A practice area, caddy cars
and catering facilities are
available.
Visitors are welcome by
arrangement.
Secretary:
Mr. W.C. McArthur -

Tel: (01786) 464098/461348.
Professional: Mr. I. Collins -
Tel: (01786) 471490.

SUTHERLAND
Bonar Bridge

**Bonar Bridge-Ardgay Golf
Club**
Bonar Bridge.
9 holes, length of course
4626 yds.
SSS Men   63,
        Ladies 66.
Charges: £10 daily, £50 weekly.
For advance reservations Tel:
(01863) 766375 (groups only).
Visitors are welcome all week.
Joint Secretaries: A. Turner -
Tel: (01549) 421248.
F. Mussard -
Tel: (01863) 766375.

Brora

Brora Golf Club
Golf Road,
Brora KW9 6QS.
Tel: (01408) 621417.
18 holes, length of course
6110 yds.
SSS 69
Charges: £18 round, £24 per
day,
£70 per week. £10 after 6pm
and during winter months.
For advance reservations Tel:
(01408) 621417.
Caddy cars, practice area and
catering facilities
(May-August) are available.
Visitors are welcome all week.
Visitors can compete in any of
our open competitions
provided they have a current
certificate of handicap with
them.
Secretary: James Fraser -
Tel: (01408) 621417.

Dornoch

Royal Dornoch Golf Club
Golf Road,
Dornoch IV25 3LW.
Web Site:
HTTP://WWW.CALI.CO.UK/RDGC

Championship Course
Tel: (01862) 810219.
18 holes, length of course
5958m/6514 yds.
Charges: On application.
For advance reservations Tel:
(01862) 810219.
Fax: (01862) 810792.
It is advisable to book.
Handicap
certificates required.
Caddies, caddy cars, practice
area and catering facilities are
available.
Visitors are welcome all week.
Secretary: John S. Duncan -
Tel: (01862) 811220.
Professional: W.E. Skinner -
Tel: (01862) 810902.

The Struie Course
18 holes, length of course
4990m/5438 yds.
Par 69
SSS 66
Charges: on request.
Caddies, caddy cars and
practice facilities.
For advance reservations -
Tel: (01862) 810219.
Fax: (01862) 810792.
Visitors welcome all week.
Secretary: John S. Duncan -
Tel: (01862) 811220.
Professional: W.E. Skinner -
Tel: (01862) 810902.

Durness

Durness Golf Club
Durness IV27 4PN.
9 holes, length of course
5545 yds/5040m.
SSS 68
Charges: On Application.
For advance reservations
Tel: (01971) 511364 or 511351.
Caddy cars, practice area and
catering facilities are available.
Visitors are welcome all week.
Secretary: Mrs. Lucy Mackay -
Tel: (01971) 511364.

Golspie

Golspie Golf Club
Ferry Road, Golspie.
Tel: (01408) 633266.
Fax: (01408) 633393.
18 holes, length of course
5337m/5836 yds.

SSS 68 (Gents)
SSS 71 (Ladies)
Charges: Weekdays £18 round.
£20 day. Weekends & Bank
Hols. £18 round, £25 Day. 5
Day Ticket: Adults £60, Junior
£25.
Package deals for parties of 10
or more - contact secretary.
Parties must book in advance.
A practice area, caddy cars
and catering facilities are
available.
Secretary: Mrs. Marie
MacLeod.

Helmsdale

Helmsdale Golf Club
Golf Road,
Helmsdale KW8 6JA.
Tel: (01431) 821339.
Length of course 3720 yds
(2 x 9 holes).
SSS 60
Charges: On Application.
Advance reservations not
necessary.
Visitors and new members are
welcome all week.
Secretary: D. Bishop.

WIGTOWNSHIRE
Glenluce

Wigtownshire County Golf Club
Mains of Park, Glenluce,
Newton Stewart.
Tel: (01581) 300420.
18 holes, length of course
5344m/5847 yds.
SSS 68
Charges: £17.50 per round,
£22 daily (weekdays).
£19.50 per round, £24 daily
(Sat/Sun & Bank Hols.).
For advance reservations
Tel: (01581) 300420.
Catering facilities are
available.
Visitors are welcome all week
except Wednesdays after
5.30pm.
Secretary: R. McKnight -
Tel: (01581) 300532.

Newton Stewart
Newton Stewart Golf Club
Kirroughtree Avenue,
Minnigaff, Newton Stewart.

Tel: (01671) 402172.
18 holes, length of course
5588m/5970 yds.
SSS 70
Charges: £17 per round, £20
daily midweek. £20 per round,
£24 daily weekends and public
holidays. £90 per week.
For advance reservations Tel:
(01671) 402172.
Catering facilities are
available.
Visitors are welcome all week.
Secretary: J. Tait -
Tel: (01671) 402172
(Clubhouse)
(01671) 403376 (Home)

Portpatrick
Portpatrick (Dunskey) Golf Club
Portpatrick DG9 8TB.
Tel: (01776) 810273.
18 holes Dunskey Course,
9 holes Dinvin Course.
Charges: Dunskey - £18
round, £27 daily (Mon-Fri).
£21 round, £32 daily
(Sat/Sun). £75 weekly.
Handicap Certificate required -
Booking advisable.
Dinvin - £8 round (18 holes),
£26 daily. No Handicap
Certificate or booking required.
Juniors under 18 half stated
price.
Secretary: J.A. Horberry -
Tel: (01776) 810273.

Port William
St. Medan Golf Club
Monreith, Port William.
Tel: (01988) 700358.
9 holes, length of course
2277 yds.
SSS 63
Charges: £12 round/daily, £15
daily, £45
weekly.
Catering facilities are
available.
Visitors are welcome all week.
Secretary: D. O'Neill -
Tel: (01988) 500555.

Stranraer

Stranraer Golf Club
Creachmore, Leswalt,
Stranraer.
Tel: (01776) 870245.

Booking advisable.
Practice area, caddy cars and catering facilities are available.
Secretary: Mr. B. C. Kelly - Tel: (01776) 870245.

Wigtown

Wigtown & Bladnoch Golf Club
Wigtown, Newton Stewart.
Tel: (01988) 403354.
9 holes, length of course 2521m.
SSS 67
Charges: £10 round, £40 weekly.
Catering facilities are available April to Sept inc.
Visitors are welcome all week.
Secretary: J. Alexander - Tel: (01988) 403209.

ISLANDS
Blackwaterfoot
Isle of Arran
Shiskine Golf and Tennis Club
Blackwaterfoot,
Isle of Arran.
Tel: (01770) 860226.
12 holes, length of course 3000 yds.
SSS 42
Charges: On Application.
Eating facilities available (June to September inc.).
Visitors are welcome.
Secretary: Mrs. F. Crawford - Tel: (01770) 860293.
Treasurer: E. Faulkner - Tel: (01770) 860392.

Brodick
Isle of Arran
Brodick Golf Club
Brodick, Isle of Arran.
Tel: (01770) 302349.
18 holes, length of course 4736 yds.
SSS 65
Charges: (1996) £10 round, £15 (Sat/Sun). £15 daily, £20 (Sat/Sun). Weekly £50.
For advance reservations Tel: (01770) 302513.
A practice area, caddy cars and catering facilities are available.

Visitors are welcome; parties by advance reservation with secretary.
Secretary: Mr. H.M. MacRae.
Professional: Mr. P.S. McCalla - Tel: (01770) 302513.

Machrie Bay Golf Club
Machrie Bay, by Brodick,
Isle of Arran.
Tel: (01770) 850232.
9 holes, length of course 1957m/2143 yds.
SSS 64
Charges: £5 round, £7.50 daily. £20 weekly.
Catering facilities are available -no bar.
Visitors are welcome all week.
Secretary: John Milesi - Tel: (01770) 850247.

Corrie
Isle of Arran
Corrie Golf Club
Sannox, Isle of Arran.
Tel: (01770) 810223.
9 holes, length of course 1948 yds.
SSS 61
Charges: On Application.
Catering facilities are available in the summer only.
Visitors are welcome all week except Saturdays.
Secretary: R. Stevenson.

Craignure
Isle of Mull
Craignure Golf Club
Craignure, Isle of Mull,
Argyll PA65 6AY.
Tel: (01680) 300402/812487.
9 holes, length of course 5072 yds.
SSS 65
Charges: £11 per day (1997)
Visitors welcome.
Course open all year.
Clubhouse open all day during summer.

Kingarth
Isle of Bute
Bute Golf Club
Kingarth.
Tel: (01700) 504369.
9 holes, length of course 2284m/2497 yds.
SSS 64

Charges: On Application.
Secretary: I. McDougall..

Kirkwall
Orkney
Orkney Golf Club
Grainbank.
Tel: (01856) 872487.
18 holes, length of course 5406 yds.
SSS 67
Charges: £10 per day at all times
A practice area is available.
Visitors are welcome all week.
Secretary: L.F. Howard - Tel: (01856) 874165.

Lamlash
Isle of Arran
Lamlash Golf Club
Tel: Clubhouse (01770) 600296.
Starter (01770) 600196.
18 holes, length of course 4640 yds.
SSS 64
Charges: £10 round Mon-Fri, £12 round Sat/Sun. £14 Day Mon-Fri, £18 Day Sat/Sun. Weekly £50. (1997).
Secretary: J. Henderson - Tel: (01770) 600272.

Lerwick
Shetland
The Shetland Golf Club
Dale Golf Course
P.O. Box 18,
Lerwick.
Tel: (01595) 840369.
18 holes, length of course 5279m/5776 yds.
SSS 70
Charges: On Application.
Visitors are welcome.
Secretary: D.C. Gray.

Lochranza
Isle of Arran
Lochranza Golf Course
Isle of Arran KA27 8HL.
Tel/Fax: (01770) 830273.
18 holes, length of course 5500 yds.
Par 70
'Play & Pay' 7 days.
Open 2nd Sun. May-end Sept.
Visitors always welcome.

Machrie
Isle of Islay

The Machrie Golf Club
The Machrie Hotel
& Golf Club,
Port Ellen, Islay
PA42 7AN.
Tel: (01496) 302310.
(Further details on
application).

Millport
Isle of Cumbrae

Millport Golf Club
Golf Road, Millport, Isle of
Cumbrae KA28 0HB.
Tel: (01475) 530311.
Length of course 5831 yds.
SSS 69
Charges: On application.
Full catering facilities are
available.
Visitors are welcome all week
without introduction.
Secretary: J. T. McGill -
Tel: (01475) 530306.
Starter: Tel: (01475) 530305.
Professional: K. Docherty -
Tel: (01475) 530305.

Port Bannantyne
Isle of Bute

Port Bannantyne Golf Club
Bannantyne Mains Road,
Port Bannantyne.
Tel: (01700) 504544.
13 holes, length of course
4653m/5085 yds.
SSS 67
Charges: On Application.
For advance reservations Tel:
(01700) 502009.
Visitors are welcome all week.
Secretary:
Mr. Ian L. MacLeod -
Tel: (01700) 502009.

Rothesay
Isle of Bute

Rothesay Golf Club
Canada Hill,
Rothesay.
Tel: (01700) 502244.
18 holes, length of course
5370 yds.
Charges: On application (day

tickets only).
Pre-booking for parties
essential Saturday/Sunday.
Full catering available.
All bookings to the:
Professional: J. Dougal -
Tel: (01700) 503554.

Scarinish
Isle of Tiree

Vaul Golf Club
Scarinish PA77 6XH.
9 holes, length of course
2911 yds.
SSS 70 (18 holes).
Secretary:
Mrs. P. Campbell -
Tel: (01879) 220334.
(Further details on
application).

Sconser
Isle of Skye

Isle of Skye Golf Club
Sconser.
9 holes, length of course
4677 yds.
SSS 64
Charges:£10 per Day including
Weekends.
Visitors welcome all week.
Secretary: M. Macdonald -
Tel: (01478) 650235.

Skeabost Bridge
Isle of Skye

Skeabost Golf Club
Skeabost House Hotel,
Skeabost Bridge
IV51 9NP.
Tel: (01470) 532215.
9 holes, length of course
1597 yds.
SSS 29
Charges: On Application.
For advanced reservations
Tel: (01470) 532215.
Catering facilities are
available.
Visitors are welcome all week.
Secretary: John Stuart -
Tel: (01470) 532322.

South Uist
Western Isles

Links-Land Golf Course
Askernish Golf Club
Askernish.
Tel: (01878) 700541.
(Further details on
application).

Stornoway
Isle of Lewis

Stornoway Golf Course
Lady Lever Park,
Stornoway HS2 OXP.
Tel: (01851) 702240.

HOTELS & GUEST HOUSES

Addresses	Type of Accommodation	Number of Rooms	Room Facilities	Packed Lunches	Season Dates	Prices p.p. B & B or B.B.E.M.	Special Features
ANGUS **Arbroath** Laura Osborne (Mrs.), "Hilltop", St. Vigeans, by Arbroath, Angus, DD11 4RD. Tel: (01241) 873200.	Guest House Highly Comm. Listed	4	Private bathrooms Public/ Shower 2 twins/ double 2 singles	Yes	All year	B. & B. £20 sharing £25 single	Superb B & B in rural setting near Letham Grange & Carnoustie. Ideal base for golfers. T.V. C.H. Tea/coffee facilities. Ample parking.
Carnoustie R. Reyner (Mr.), Park House, 12 Park Avenue, Carnoustie, Angus DD7 7JA. Tel: (01241) 852101.	Victorian Guest House 2 Crowns Highly Comm.	4	All with colour T.V., Tea/ Coffee facilities some en-suite	Yes	All year	B. & B. from £20.	Comfortable Victorian villa, 5 minutes from golf course. Non smoking.
Dundee Heather Flynn (Miss), Ballinard House Hotel, 26 Claypotts Road, Broughty Ferry, Dundee DD5 1BU Angus. Tel: (01382) 739555.	Hotel 4 Crowns.	40	Tea/Coffee facilities Iron	Yes	All year	B. & B. £25-£29.45 B.B.E.M. £35-£39.45	Victorian house set in four acres of mature gardens. Satellite T.V. Trouser press. Telephone.
Jon Stewart (Mr), The Fisherman's Tavern & Hotel, 10-14 Fort Street, Broughty Ferry, Dundee, Angus. Tel: (01382) 775941.	Hotel Listed Comm.	8	Tea/Coffee facilities Sky T.V.	Yes	All year	B. & B. £17-£21 p.p.p.n.	Consumers Association "Which?" Recommended for bar food. Camra National Pub of the Year.
ARGYLL **Campbeltown** McLean (Mr), The Delwood Hotel, Drumore, Campbeltown, Argyll PA28 6HD. Tel: (01586) 552465	Hotel 3 Crowns Comm.	12	10 en-suite	Yes	All year	B. & B. from £16-25 Dinner £8	Family run secluded hotel situated near Machrihanish. Home made delicious food. Very warm welcome. Honeymoon suite.

Addresses	Type of Accommodation	Number of Rooms	Room Facilities	Packed Lunches	Season Dates	Prices p.p. B & B or B.B.E.M.	Special Features
Isle of Gigha S. Howden (Mrs.), Gigha Hotel, Isle of Gigha, Argyll PA41 7AA. Tel: (01583) 505254. Fax: (01583) 505244.	Hotel 4 Crowns Comm.	13	T. V. Telephone En-suite	Ask	Mar-Oct	B.B.E.M. £57 p.p.	Nearby Achamore gardens and 9 hole golf course with beautiful views.
Oban C. MacDonald (Mrs.), Bracker, Polvinister Road, Oban, Argyll PA34 5TN. Tel: (01631) 564302.	Guest House 2 Crown Comm.	3	En-suite Tea/Coffee facilities T.V.	No	Mar-Nov	B. & B. £16-£18	Beautiful quiet location. Private parking. Non smoking.
Strachur Anderson (Mr.), Creggans Inn, Strachur, Argyll PA27 8BX. Tel: (01369) 860279.	Inn 3 Crowns Comm.	19	All en-suite T.V. Telephone	£8.50	Feb-Dec	B. & B. £45 B.B.E.M.. £64	Overlooking Loch Fyne. Three superb golf courses within 20 miles.
AYRSHIRE **Ayr** Reservations & Information, Elms Court Hotel, 21 Miller Road, Ayr, Ayrshire KA7 2AX. Tel: (01292) 264191/ 282332 Fax: (01292) 610254.	Hotel 4 Crowns Comm.	20	20	Yes	All year	B. & B. from £30-£40 p.p. B.B.E.M. from £45-£55 p.p.	Popular town centre hotel, free parking & entry to local fitness centre. Excellent food & service.
G. Anton (Mrs), Clyde Cottage, 1 Arran Terrace, Ayr, Ayrshire KA7 1JF. Tel: (01292) 267368.	Guest House 2 Crowns Comm.	3	All wash hand basins 1 en-suite	Ask	All year	B. & B. from £16	Private parking. 5 mins. town centre. 200 yards from esplanade. T.V. all rooms. Tea making facilities.
Julia Clark, Eglinton Guest House, 23 Eglinton Terrace, Ayr, Ayrshire. Tel/Fax: (01292) 264623.	Guest House 1 Crown Comm.	8	En-suite available Colour T.V. Tea/Coffee facilities C.H.	Yes	All year	B. & B. £17.00 p.p.p.n.	For golfing enthusiasts, Turnberry and Royal Troon are only a short distance away. There are many good golf courses nearby.

Addresses	Type of Accommodation	Number of Rooms	Room Facilities	Packed Lunches	Season Dates	Prices p.p. B & B or B.B.E.M.	Special Features
Ayr R.Gibson (Mr & Mrs), Iona Guest House, 27 St. Leonards Road, Ayr, Ayrshire KA7 2PS. Tel: (01292) 269541.	Guest House 2 Crowns Comm.	4	2 en-suite Tea/Coffee facilities Radio alarm	Ask	Feb - Nov	B. & B. single £16-£18 double/twin £16-£18	Easy drive to 20 courses. Walking distance to town centre. Private parking. Drying facilities. Residents lounge.
Prestwick Iain W. Gray (Mr), Kincraig Hotel, 39 Ayr Road, Prestwick, Ayrshire. Tel/Fax: (01292) 479480.	Hotel	8	En-suite	No	All year	B. & B. from £21 p.p. Evening meals by prior arrangement	Ideally situated for all the nearby Championship courses.
Troon K. Ronney (Mrs), The Anchorage Hotel, 149 Templehill, Troon, Ayrshire KA10 6BQ. Tel: (01292) 317448.	Hotel Fully licensed Award pending	11	1 family room 1 four poster bed All en-suite	Yes	All year	Weekend B. & B. £15 Midweek B. & B. £12.50	Great hotel, great location, comfortable - what more is required? Colour T.V. Radio alarm. Telephone. Tea/coffee facilities.
BERWICKSHIRE **Lauder** Jo Sutherland (Mrs), The Lodge at Carfraemill, Lauder, Berwickshire TD2 6RA. Tel: (01578) 750750.	Hotel 4 Crowns Highly Comm.	10	All en-suite single doubles family	Yes	All year	B. & B. from £35	Most attractive country lodge within half an hour of many golf courses. Colour T.V., satellite, tea/coffee facilities.
CLACKMANNANSHIRE **Alloa** Yvonne McGregor (Mrs), Claremont Lodge Hotel, 23 Kellie Place, Alloa, Clackmannanshire. Tel: (01259) 214575.	Hotel 3 Crowns Comm.	10	All en-suite T.V. Telephone Tea/Coffee facilities	Yes	All year	B. & B. Single £34 Double £54	Many excellent golf courses within easy reach. Friendly, comfortable hotel with new conservatory. Excellent home cooking.
DUMFRIESSHIRE **Dumfries** G. Ford (Mr & Mrs), Brae House Country Guest House, Crocketford Road (A75), Crocketford, Dumfriesshire DG2 8QE. Tel: (01556) 690253.	Guest House 2 Crowns Comm.	3	En-suite bathrooms T.V. Tea/Coffee making facilities	Yes	All year round	B. & B. £18 B.B.E.M. £28	Charming 18th century country house with wonderful views over Galloway hills. 7 miles from Dumfries. Easy reach of many golf courses.

Addresses	Type of Accommodation	Number of Rooms	Room Facilities	Packed Lunches	Season Dates	Prices p.p. B & B or B.B.E.M.	Special Features
Kirkcudbright M. Chierici (Mrs), Gordon House Hotel, High Street, Kirkcudbright, Dumfriesshire DG6 4JQ. Tel: (01557) 330670.	Hotel 1 Crown Approved	12		Yes	All year	B.B.E.M. £29 p.p.	2 bars, pool table.
Lockerbie Tindal (Mr & Mrs), Ravenshill House Hotel, 12 Dumfries Road, Lockerbie, Dumfriesshire. Tel: (01576) 202882.	Hotel 3 Crowns Comm.	8	En-suite Colour T.V. Radio Telephone Tea/Coffee C.H.	Ask	All Year	B. & B. twin £25.00 p.p. B.B.E.M. twin £32.00 p.p.	Good food, comfortable accommodation. Numerous courses. Groups catered for.
Carry (Mrs), Kings Arms Hotel, High Street, Lockerbie, Dumfriesshire. Tel/Fax: (01576) 202410.	Hotel 3 Crowns.	14	En-suite T.V. Hospitality trays etc. Direct dial telephones.	Yes	All year	B. & B. £27.50 double/twin £30.00 single p.p.	Log fires. A la carte restaurant. Traditional Coaching Inn.
Moniaive Robin McIver (Mr), Woodlea Hotel, Moniaive, Dumfriesshire DG3 4EN. Tel: (01848) 200209.	Hotel 3 Crowns Comm.	12	Private bath Hairdryer Mini-bar Tea/Coffee facilities	Yes	Easter- end Oct	B & B from £25.00 B.B.E.M. £55.00	Stay 3 nights for free golf. Swimming pool. Tennis. Bikes. Ponies.
FIFE **Ladybank** J.S. McGregor (Mr & Mrs), Redlands Country Lodge, by Ladybank, Fife KY15 7SH. Tel/ Fax: (01337) 831091.	Guest House Awaiting Inspection	4	All en-suite Tea/Coffee facilities colour T.V. C.H. Hairdyers	Ask	Mar- Nov	B. & B. £20-£22 B.B.E.M. £30-£32	Norwegian pine lodge in countryside setting. Ideal centre for golf and touring. Weekly terms available.
St. Andrews Scores Hotel, 76, The Scores, St. Andrews, Fife KY16 9BB. Tel: (01334) 472451. Fax: (01334) 473947.	Hotel 4 Crowns Comm.	30	All rooms en-suite T.V./radio Trouser press Tea/Coffee facilities	No	Nov- Mar	B. & B. from £36.00 April from £54 May-Oct from £68.00	Adjacent to golf courses and short stroll to town centre.

Addresses	Type of Accommodation	Number of Rooms	Room Facilities	Packed Lunches	Season Dates	Prices p.p. B & B or B.B.E.M.	Special Features
St. Andrews Kornelia Inverarity (Mrs), Fossil House & Cottage, 14 Main Street, Strathkinness, St. Andrews, Fife KY16 9RU. Tel: (01334) 850639.	Guest House 3 Crowns Highly Comm.	4	All en-suite 2 twin 1 double 1 family	No	All year	B. & B. £20-£25	Self contained luxury accommodation. All rooms have colour T.V., fridge. hairdryer, trouser press, welcome tray and fresh fruit. Guest house and conservatory. Garden and car park.
INVERNESS-SHIRE **Strathglass** Hugh Stanford (Mr.), Tomich Hotel, Strathglass, Inverness-shire IV4 7LY. Tel: (01456) 415399.	Hotel 4 Crowns Highly Comm.	8	En-suite T.V. Tea/Coffee making facilities		All year	B. & B. £25-£45	Indoor swimming pool, fishing, bike hire, walking, good restaurant.
KIRKCUDBRIGHTSHIRE **Gatehouse of Fleet** Murray Arms Hotel, High Street, Gatehouse of Fleet, Castle Douglas, Kirkcudbrightshire. Tel: (01557) 814207.	Hotel 3 Crown Comm.	13	All en-suite Colour T.V. Tea/Coffee facilities D.D. phones. C.H.	Yes	All year	B. & B. from £45 B.B.E.M. £57.50	Warm, welcoming historic Inn. Good food available all day.
LOTHIANS **Edinburgh** M. Urquhart (Mrs), Kildonan Lodge, 27 Craigmillar Park, Edinburgh. Tel: 0131-667 2793. Fax: 0131-667 9777.	Guest House 2 Crowns Highly Comm.	12	All en-suite	Ask	All year.	B. & B. from £28-£40	Beautifully restored lodge. Excellent location for golf. Car park. Licensed.
Y. Livornese (Mrs), 22 West Mayfield, Edinburgh EH9 1TQ. Tel: 0131-667 1241.	Guest House Approved Listed	6	4 en-suite 2 basic.	Yes	All year	B. & B. Double/twin en-suite from £22-£25 basic £18-£22 single £25-£35	City centre close to both bus & train station. Car park.
Musselburgh A.R.Mitchell (Miss), Craigesk, 10 Albert Terrace, Musselburgh East Lothian EH21 7LR. Tel: 0131-665 3344/3170. Fax: 0131-665 3344.	Guest House 1 Crown Approved	4	2 twin 2 family W.H.B. C. T.V. Radio/ alarms Tea/Coffee facilities C.H. Payphone	No	All year	B. & B. from £16	Near all East Lothian golf courses. 20 minutes from Edinburgh. Private parking.

Addresses	Type of Accommodation	Number of Rooms	Room Facilities	Packed Lunches	Season Dates	Prices p.p. B & B or B.B.E.M.	Special Features
North Berwick Chalmers (Mr.), Tantallon Inn, 4 Marine Parade, North Berwick, Lothians. Tel: (01620) 892238.	Hotel	4	Colour T.V. W.H.B. Tea/Coffee facilities	No	All year	B. & B. from £22.00	Beach front hotel. 800 yards from Glen Golf Course.
Threemiletown Carol Jones. The Kennels, Threemiletown, West Lothian. Tel/Fax: (01506) 834200. Mobile: 0831 893954	Guest House Comm.	5	En-suite T.V. Tea/Coffee facilities	Yes	All year	B. & B. £18-£30	Farmhouse/central/10 mins airport/bus route/garden. Dogs & cats etc. welcome.
MORAYSHIRE **Grantown on Spey** Still (Mr), Strathspey Hotel, High Street, Grantown on Spey, Morayshire. Tel: (01479) 872002.	Hotel 3 Crowns Comm.	6	En-suite Colour T.V. Tea/Coffee facilities C.H. Car park Payphone	Yes	All year.	B. & B. from £20 -£25 B.B.E.M. £32-£37.	Central location. Ideal base for many excellent golf courses. Excellent food.
PERTHSHIRE **Blairgowrie** Angela Stevenson (Mrs), Kintrae House Hotel, Balmoral Road, Blairgowrie, Perthshire. Tel: (01250) 872106.	Hotel Awaiting new gradings	5	All en-suite Colour T.V.s Tea/Coffee facilities	Yes	All year	B. & B. from £20 p.p.	Small family run hotel. Excellent cuisine. Heart of golf country.
G. & S. McPherson (Mr & Mrs), The Laurels, Golf Course Road, Rosemount, Blairgowrie, Perthshire. Tel: (01250) 874920.	Guest House Highly Comm. 3 Crowns	6	En-suite Tea/Coffee	Yes	Mid Jan- end Nov	B. & B. £19.00 p.p.p.n.	Within easy distance of many lovely courses. We will provide you with first class food with a la carte dinner.
G.C.Mitchell (Mr), Royal Hotel, 53 Allan Street, Blairgowrie, Perthshire. Tel: (01250) 872226.	Hotel 3 Crowns.	47	31	Yes	All year	On application	A Georgian fronted hotel privately owned and situated in the town centre. Car and coach park. Children welcome.
Coupar Angus John Broadley (Mr), St. Catherines Croft, 14 Union Street, Coupar Angus, Perthshire. PH13 9AE.	Victorian House 2 Crowns Comm.	4	2 en-suite H. & C. T.V. C.H. Tea/Coffee facilities	Yes	All year.	B. & B. £16-£20	Family run. Comfortable rooms. Drying facilities. Ample car parking.

Tel: (01828) 627753.

Addresses	Type of Accommodation	Number of Rooms	Room Facilities	Packed Lunches	Season Dates	Prices p.p. B & B or B.B.E.M.	Special Features
Coupar Angus Alan Robson (Mr), Royal Hotel, The Cross, Coupar Angus, Perthshire PH13 9DA. Tel: (01828) 627549.	Hotel	7	Shower W.H. Tea/Coffee facilities T.V.	Yes	All year	B. & B. £17.00 B.B.E.M. £22.00	Close to a number of golf courses. Fishing is also available.
Crieff A. Hoskins (Mrs), Leven House Hotel, Comrie Road, Crieff, Perthshire PH7 4BA. Tel: (01764) 652529.	Hotel 2 Crowns Comm.	10	En-suite Colour T.V. Tea/Coffee facilities Lounge	Yes	All year	B. & B. £16 - £22 H.T. £7.50 Dinner £12.00	Friendly family hotel. Centrally located 12 courses. From £9 per day.
Dunkeld Chalmers (Mr), Birnam House Hotel, Perth Road, Birnam, Dunkeld, Perthshire PH8 0BQ. Tel: (01350) 727462.	Hotel 3 Crowns Comm.	28	En-suite C.T.V. D.D. telephones	Yes	All year	B. & B. £32-£45 single £25-£35 double/twin	Set in the ancient village of Macbeth lies the Birnam House Hotel. Ideal base for golf, fishing, touring and relaxing.
Kinloch Rannoch Jennifer Skeaping (Mrs), Bunrannoch House, Kinloch Rannoch, Perthshire PH16 5QB. Tel: (01882) 632407.	Guest House 2 Crowns Comm.	7	2 family 3 double en-suite 2 twin sharing	Yes	Open all year except Xmas/ New Year	B. & B. £19.00 p.p.p.n.	Spacious, comfortable home. Warm welcome. Good cooking.
Kinross Stephen H. Whiting (Mr), Glenfarg Hotel & Restaurant, Main Street, Glenfarg, Perthshire. Tel: (01577) 830241.	Hotel 3 Crowns Comm.	17	En-suite Tea / Coffee facilities Colour T.V. Direct dial telephones	Yes	All year	B. & B. from £20 B.B.E.M. £29.50	Popular & friendly village hotel. Golfing package specialists. Riverside beer garden.
Perth E. D. Anderson (Mr), Grampian Hotel, 37 York Place, Perth, Perthshire PA2 8EA. Tel: (01738) 621057.	Hotel 3 Crowns	14	En-suite Cable T.V. Tea/Coffee facilities Direct dial telephones	Yes	All year	B. & B. £29	Within range of many excellent courses. 2 minutes walk from Perth city centre.

Addresses	Type of Accommodation	Number of Rooms	Room Facilities	Packed Lunches	Season Dates	Prices p.p. B & B or B.B.E.M.	Special Features
Pitlochry D. Spaven (Mr), Atholl Palace Hotel, Pitlochry, Perthshire PH16 5LY. Tel: (01796) 472400.	Hotel 4 Crowns Comm.	76	Yes	Yes	All year	B. & B. from £35	Baronial style building in 48 acres including 9 hole pitch n' putt.
F. Norris (Mrs), Kinnaird House, Kirkmichael Road, Pitlochry, Perthshire PH16 5JL. Tel: (01796) 472843.	Guest House 2 Crowns Highly Comm.	3	All en-suite	No	Mar - Oct	B. & B. £20-£25	Quality accommodation in superb Victorian villa. Cottage also available.
ROXBURGHSHIRE **Jedburgh** Jenny Bywater, "Glenfriars" Country House, The Friars, Jedburgh, Roxburghshire TD8 6BN. Tel/Fax: (01835) 862000.	Country House 3 Crowns Comm.	6	All en-suite	Yes	All year except Xmas & New Year	B. & B. £32-£35 Evening meal from £15.00	Georgian house in lovely quiet side of town. Wonderful cooking by Jenny Bywater.
Melrose Michael Dalgetty (Mr), Kings Arms Hotel, High Street, Melrose, Roxburghshire. Tel: (01896) 822143.	Hotel 3 Crowns Comm.	6	3 shower 3 bath en-suite	Yes	All year	B. & B. £26.75 - £33 p.p.	One of Scotland's oldest coaching inns offering superb value.
St. Boswells A. Johnstone (Mr & Mrs), The Clachan, Main Street, St. Boswells, Melrose, Roxburghshire TD6 0BG. Tel: (01835) 822266.	Guest House 2 Crowns Comm.	4	Private bathroom En-suite 2 twin 2 single	£3.50 p.p.	Mar-Oct	B. & B. £20 p.p. No evening meal	Freedom of the fairways. Golf package 3/5 days. Pass available only £7 per round..
SELKIRKSHIRE **Galashiels** Scott (Mrs), Abbotsford Arms Hotel, 63 Stirling Street, Galashiels, Selkirkshire TD1 1BY. Tel: (01896) 752517. Fax: (01896) 750744.	Hotel 3 Crowns	14	10	Yes	All year	B. & B. £28 - £36	Family run hotel serving excellent food.

Addresses	Type of Accommodation	Number of Rooms	Room Facilities	Packed Lunches	Season Dates	Prices p.p. B & B or B.B.E.M.	Special Features
SUTHERLAND **Assynt** A. H. Archibald (Mrs), Inchnadamph Hotel, Assynt by Lairg, Sutherland IV27 4HN. Tel: (01571) 822202.	Hotel S.T.B Grading pending	23	10 en-suite other rooms with W.H.B.	Yes	All year	B. & B. £39 B.B.E.M. £49	Fishing for salmon and brown trout free to hotel guests.
WIGTOWNSHIRE **Glenluce** Ian Holmes (Mr), Kelvin House Hotel, 53 Main Street, Glenluce, Wigtownshire DG8 0PP. Tel/Fax: (01581) 300303.	Hotel 3 Crowns Comm.	6	4 en-suite T.V. Tea/Coffee facilities Telephone	Yes	All year	B. & B. from £20.00	Golf parties our speciality. Concessionary rates for golf. Pleasant tranquil village. Close to ferry terminals and seacat. Taste of Scotland recommended.
ISLE OF ARRAN **Brodick** Thompson (Mr & Mrs), Carrick Lodge, Brodick, Isle of Arran KA27 8BH. Tel: (01770) 302550.	Guest House 3 Crowns Comm.	6	En-suite Colour T.V. Hairdryers Clock radio C.H.	Yes	Feb - Oct	B. & B. £23.00 B.B.E.M. £35	Old sandstone manse in own grounds with panoramic views.
Lamlash June Shankland, Aldersyde Hotel, Shore Road, Lamlash, Isle of Arran. Tel: (01770) 600219.	Hotel S.T.B. Grading Pending	14	Tea/Coffee facilities H & C	Ask	All year	B & B from £15	Excellent location for golf. Discount given for party bookings for over one night.
Whiting Bay C. A.Wannop (Mrs), Kiscadale Hotel, Whiting Bay, Isle of Arran KA27 8PR. Tel: (01770) 700236.	Licensed Hotel Award pending	8	Hand basins Tea/Coffee facilities	Ask	All year	B. & B. £17.00	Glorious views across bay. 5 minute walk to golf course.
ISLE OF SKYE **Sligachan** C. A. Wannop (Mrs), Kiscadale Hotel, Whiting Bay, Isle of Arran, KA27 8PR. Tel: (01770) 700236.	Hotel 3 Crowns Comm.	22	En-suite T.V. Tea/Coffee facilities	Yes	All year	B. & B. from £35 Winter rates £20.00	Glorious views across bay. 5 minute walk to golf course.

SELF CATERING

Addresses	Type of Accommodation	Number of Units	Number Sleeping	Shop Near	Season Dates	Prices Per Unit.	Special Features
ANGUS **Carnoustie** Write to: Douglas W. B. Milne (Mr), 11 Little Carron Gardens, St. Andrews, Fife KY16 8QL. Tel: (01334) 479821.	Ground floor flat 4 Crowns Comm.	1	4	Yes	Jan - Dec	£150-£275	Directly opposite 18th green. Spacious and comfortable. Own parking. Pets welcome.
AYRSHIRE **Ballantrae** Drummond (Mrs), Ardstinchar Cottage, Ballantrae, Ayrshire KA26 0NA. Tel: (01465) 831343.	Cottage 4 Crowns Comm.	3	6	2 miles	Jan-Dec	£130-£240	Luxury cottage, fully equipped set in panoramic countryside. Home from home.
BANFFSHIRE **Buckie** The Manager, Letterfourie, Buckie, Banffshire AB56 2JP. Tel: (01542) 832298.	Flats 5 Crowns Comm.	1	3	3 miles	All year	£180-£630 weekly	10 local courses. Private 300 acre estate. Tennis court.
FIFE **Cupar** M. Chrisp (Mrs), Scotstarvit Farm, Cupar, Fife KY15 5PA. Tel: (01334) 653591.	Cottage 4 Crowns	1	5 + cot	Yes	All year	£110-295	Stone built cottage with secluded gardens. Private parking. 30 golf courses within approx. 30 miles radius perfectly placed for many activities. Farmhouse B. & B. Hearty breakfasts. Panoramic scenery.
St. Andrews Eve Brown Property Management, 23 Argyle Street, St. Andrews, Fife KY16 9BX. Tel: (01334) 478800. Fax: (01334) 478855.	Flats Cottages Houses	36 1 27	2-12	Yes	Mid June End of Aug	£150-£440	A selection of properties in St. Andrews. Bus nearby. Rail 6 miles. Airport 12 miles.
21st Century Property & Estate Agency Ltd, 32/34 Albert Road, Glasgow G42 8DN. Tel: 0141 - 424 4444.	House/flat 1 Crown Approved 4 Crowns Comm.	3	4-6	Yes	June-Sept	£150-£350	Colour T.V. Automatic washing machine. Some have dishwasher, microwave, shower.

Addresses	Type of Accommodation	Number of Units	Number Sleeping	Shop Near	Season Dates	Prices Per Unit.	Special Features
INVERNESS-SHIRE **Boat of Garten** B. Gillies (Mr), Boat of Garten Caravan Park, Boat of Garten, Inverness-shire PH24 3BN. Tel: (01479) 831652.	Holiday Cabins Thistle 5 Ticks	5	6	Yes	All year	From £87 - £355	River Spey, golf, tennis, steam railway. All within walking distance.
KIRKCUDBRIGHTSHIRE **Castle Douglas** Ball (Mr & Mrs), Barncrosh Farm, Castle Douglas Kirkcudbrightshire DG7 1TX. Tel: (01556) 680216.	Cottages 2-4 Crown Comm.	13	2-8	5 miles	All year	On application	Enjoy a peaceful relaxing holiday on a farm near coast and hills. Fully equipped cottages and dogs welcome.
MORAYSHIRE **Lossiemouth** G. N. Kerr (Mr), Silver Sands Leisure Park, Covesea, West Beach, Lossiemouth, Morayshire IV31 6SP. Tel: (01343) 813262.	Caravans 4 Ticks	48	6/8	Yes	Mar - Oct	£110-£475	Next to Moray Golf Club. Ideal base for the many courses throughout Morayshire.
PERTHSHIRE **Bankfoot** C. McKay, Blair House, Main Street, Bankfoot, nr. Perth, Perthshire. Tel: (01738) 787338.	Cottage 5 Crowns Comm.	1	5	Yes	All year	From £200	Telephone, microwave, central heating. Washing machine. Dryer, dishwasher, fridge freezer etc.,
Blairgowrie M. Ferguson (Mrs), Fyal, Alyth, Blairgowrie, Perthshire. Tel: (01828) 632997.	Cottage 2 Crowns.	1	5	2.5 miles	All year	£200 p.w.	Two golf clubs already open. Pay and Play.
Catherine Peebles , Ericht Holiday Lodges, Balmoral Road, Blairgowrie, Perthshire. Tel: (01250) 874686. Fax: (01250) 875616.	Lodges 3 Crowns Comm. - 4 Crowns Highly Comm.	6	4-6	500 yards	All year	£180-£385	Ideally situated for golfers. 7 excellent courses, all within 15-20 minutes drive not to mention the golf courses in Perth and surrounding areas. Great accommodation with full gas central heating.

Addresses	Type of Accommodation	Number of Units	Number Sleeping	Shop Near	Season Dates	Prices Per Unit.	Special Features
Blairgowrie Margaret Wood (Mrs), Blairgowrie Holiday Park, Rattray, Blairgowrie, Perthshire PH10 7AL. Tel: (01250) 872941. Fax: (01250) 874535.	Lodges Caravans Touring Caravans 3 Crowns Highly Comm. 5 Ticks Excellent	12	2-8	Yes	All year	From £175 Touring from £7.50 p.n	Holiday homes on beautiful landscaped park. Choice of seven golf courses within 5 miles from park.
Bridge of Cally J. Farmer (Mrs), Persie Mains, Bridge of Cally, Blairgowrie, Perhshire PH10 7LQ. Tel: (01250) 886250.	Cottages 4 Crowns Highly Comm.	3	5-6	Yes	All year	£150-£350	Quality accommodation on a Highland Estate. Superb view and amenities.
Comrie Wallace Booth Snr (Mr), Loch View Farm, Mill of Fortune, Comrie, Perthshire PH6 2JE. Tel: (01764) 670677.	Detached House & Apartment Awaiting Grading	1 1	Up to 8 2	2 miles	All year	On Application £190-£250	Gleneagles-12 miles, 3 courses. Comrie-2 miles, 9 holes. Crieff-6 miles, 18 holes. Muthill-7 miles, 9 holes. St. Fillans- 6miles, 9 holes.
SUTHERLAND **Brora** P. Sowerby (Mr), c/o Mrs M. F. Sowerby, Balnacoil Cottage, Brora, Sutherland. Tel: (01408) 621219.	Cottage 4 Crowns Deluxe	1	8	Yes	All year	£295-£425 p.w.	Spectacular views. Four excellent golf courses within 10-20 minutes drive. Good walking.
WIGTOWNSHIRE **Newton Stewart** Eric Hyslop (Mr), Borgan, Bargrennan, Newton Stewart, Wigtownshire DG8 6SR. Tel: (01671) 840247.	Cottages 4 Crowns Comm.	2	4	Yes	All year	£175-£265 per cottage	Many golf courses within easy reach. Turnberry only 45 minutes away.

KEY TO MAPS

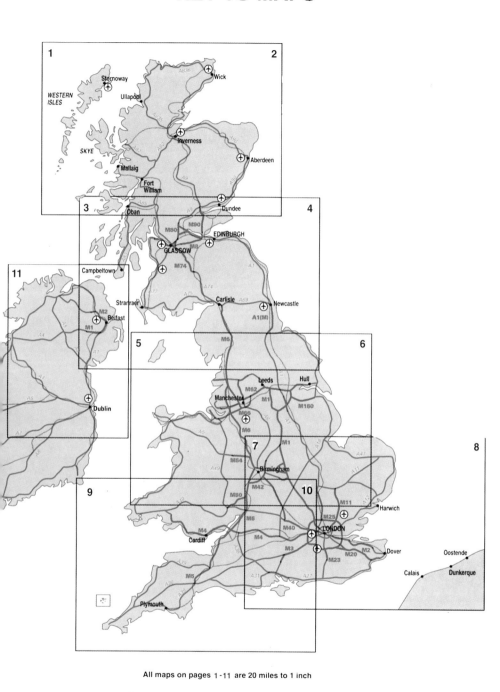

All maps on pages 1-11 are 20 miles to 1 inch

0   10   20   30   40 Miles

0   10   20   30   40   50   60 Kilometres

© Baynefield Carto-Graphics Ltd 1995

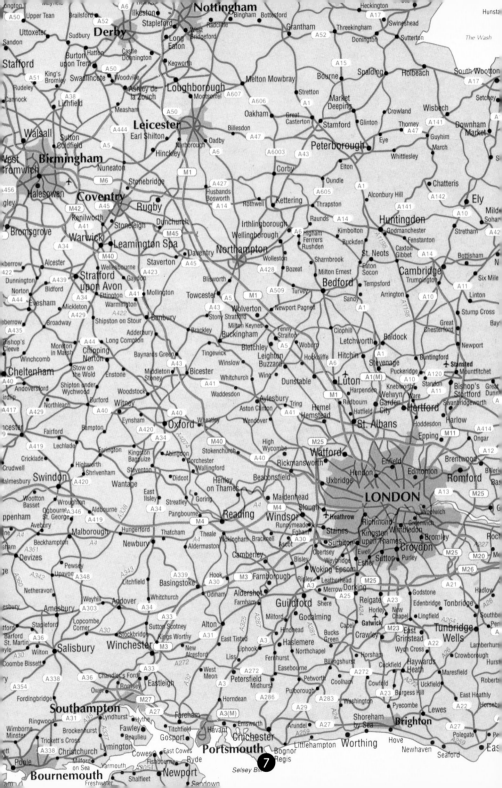

ISLES OF SCILLY

Bryher
Samson · Tresco
Hugh Town · St. Martin's
Anner · Gugh · St. Mary's
St. Agnes

9

© Baynefield Carto-Graphics Ltd. 1995

	Aberdeen	Birmingham	Bristol	Cardiff	Carlisle	Dover	Edinburgh	Fort William	Glasgow	Holyhead	Hull	Inverness	Leeds	Liverpool	London	Manchester	Newcastle	Norwich	Nottingham	Plymouth
Aberdeen	-	698	830	864	377	942	203	254	238	745	579	171	528	579	882	568	381	789	637	1017
Birmingham	434	-	142	174	319	328	480	657	478	245	225	737	195	163	193	143	333	283	85	327
Bristol	516	88	-	76	454	336	613	792	613	380	373	872	354	298	193	277	481	375	232	201
Cardiff	537	108	47	-	486	393	645	824	645	330	406	904	386	330	249	311	513	430	266	262
Carlisle	234	198	282	302	-	639	158	336	158	367	275	417	195	201	504	192	93	457	303	639
Dover	585	204	209	244	397	-	735	977	800	566	420	1059	435	484	127	463	566	274	348	468
Edinburgh	126	298	381	401	98	457	-	214	74	526	373	254	320	360	665	352	174	581	428	798
Fort William	158	408	492	512	209	607	133	-	164	705	613	105	533	539	842	529	388	795	641	977
Glasgow	148	297	381	401	98	497	46	102	-	526	435	278	356	360	665	352	248	616	462	798
Holyhead	463	152	236	205	228	352	327	438	327	-	356	785	267	166	430	198	428	494	283	565
Hull	360	140	232	252	171	261	232	381	270	221	-	694	98	209	303	159	230	243	150	558
Inverness	106	458	542	562	259	658	158	65	173	488	431	-	615	620	922	608	431	875	723	1057
Leeds	328	121	220	240	121	270	199	331	221	166	61	382	-	121	319	71	150	280	117	539
Liverpool	360	101	185	205	125	301	224	335	224	103	130	385	75	-	348	56	282	389	175	483
London	548	120	120	155	313	79	413	523	413	267	188	573	198	216	-	328	460	185	209	388
Manchester	353	89	172	193	119	288	219	329	219	123	99	379	44	35	204	-	232	299	113	463
Newcastle	237	207	299	319	58	352	108	241	154	266	143	268	93	175	286	144	-	410	257	666
Norwich	490	176	233	267	284	170	361	494	383	307	151	544	174	242	115	186	255	-	193	570
Nottingham	396	53	144	165	188	216	266	398	287	176	93	449	73	109	130	70	160	120	-	418
Plymouth	632	203	125	163	397	291	496	607	496	351	347	657	335	300	241	288	414	354	260	-

Roman Figures = Miles;   Italic Figures = Kilometres